GROUNDSWELL

First published in 2013
The Dedalus Press
13 Moyclare Road
Baldoyle
Dublin 13
Ireland

www.dedaluspress.com

Copyright © Patrick Deeley 1986, 1990, 1995, 2000, 2008, 2011, 2013

ISBN 978 1 906614 73 7 (paperback)

All rights reserved.
No part of this publication may be reproduced in any form or by any means without the prior permission of the publisher.

Dedalus Press titles are represented in the UK by
Central Books, 99 Wallis Road, London E9 5LN
and in North America by Syracuse University Press, Inc.,
621 Skytop Road, Suite 110, Syracuse, New York 13244.

Cover Painting: 'Workshop', oil on canvas,
80 x 60 cm, 2011 by Judy Carroll Deeley
www.judycarrolldeeley.com

The Dedalus Press receives financial assistance from
The Arts Council / An Chomhairle Ealaíon

GROUNDSWELL
New and Selected Poems

Patrick Deeley

DEDALUS PRESS
DUBLIN, IRELAND

ACKNOWLEDGEMENTS

Acknowledgements are due to the editors of the following, where most of the new poems here, or versions of them, first appeared: *The Irish Times; New Hibernia Review* (University of St. Thomas, Minnesota); *Crannóg Magazine; Skylight 47; Shine On* (ed. Pat Boran, Dedalus Press, 2011); *The Shop; The Stony Thursday Book; Digital Wingspan; The Oxfam Calendar 2009; Bamboo Dreams: Irish Haiku Anthology* (ed. Anatoly Kudryavitsky, Doghouse Press, 2012); *Whirligig* (Netherlands); *The Moth; Southword; The Stinging Fly; Poetry Ireland Review; The Galway Review;* and *South Bank Poetry* (London). The poems in 'The Flowing Bones' section appeared in *Le Ossa della Creazione,* a translation into Italian by Chiara de Luca, published by Edizioni Kolibris (2010). Other poems were included in an English-French edition, *Territoire,* translated by Emmanuel Malherbet and published in France by éditions alidades (2011).

Contents

Introduction by Theo Dorgan / 11

THE HIDDEN VILLAGE

Languages / 17
Dry Stone Walls / 18
The Bee Queen of Mullagh Beg / 19
Gallagh Man / 20
Dislocator / 21
Big Ned's Guest / 24
Lodger's High / 25
Minding Goal / 26
Under Clonlahan Bridge / 27
Lena Alone / 28
The Road Lorg / 29
Old John / 30
Cowdung / 31
A Man from Derrybrien / 32
Sand Quarry Skull / 33
The Old Headstones / 34
The Pictures / 35
Aughrim of the Slaughter / 36
Friends / 38
A Study in Juttings / 39
1969 / 41
The Life and Times of Oliver J Martin MEP / 42
In the Boilerhouse / 45
Emigrant / 46
October / 48
The Chalk-Face / 49

Ghost / 50
The Crucifixion of Tommy Joe / 51
Panache / 52
Axe / 53
Marigold / 54
Crank of Nature / 55
His First Word / 56

KING OF THE WOOD

Rathgar Pastoral / 59
Monkey-Puzzle / 60
Instrument / 61
The Mantle / 62
Wood Rap / 64
Hornets' Nest / 65
Burren / 66
The Antique King / 67
Sub-fossil Tree Shore / 69
Impatiens / 70
Fruit Man / 71
Nature and our Devices / 76
The Addergoole Cot / 77
To the Dryad / 79
For a Gardener / 80
Yard Sticks / 81
King of the Wood / 82
Woodman / 83
Red Sash / 86
Sap Myth / 87
Dargle Oak / 88
Pollarded Beech / 89
In Killalaghton Graveyard / 90
Names Remain / 91
The King of South Galway / 92

The Dissatisfied Youth / 93
Son of Hazel / 94
Críochán Thorn / 95
Cromlach's Deception / 96
Baile and Aillinn / 97
Ash / 98

THE FLOWING BONES

Dandelions / 101
Callows Water Barrel / 102
One of a Kind / 103
Keaveney's Well / 104
The Marl Excavations / 105
Wellspring / 106
Territory / 107
A Burrishoole Gate / 108
Muslin / 109
Frogs / 110
Capstone / 111
The Cailleach / 112
Birdsong / 114
Cave Life / 115
Species / 117
Piecework / 118
The Last Seanchaí / 120
Night / 122
Simulation / 123
Mistletoe / 125
Rocking Horse / 126
The Owl / 127
Bluebell / 128
Millennium / 130
Journey / 131
Dust / 132

The Badger on Orwell Bridge / 133
Fisherman / 134
The Bear / 136
The Roadside Crosses /138
Tuscan Afternoon / 140
Foxhall Sunset / 141
Bare Branches / 143
Le Gave / 144
Mars / 145
Ghosts / 146

FEAR BRÉIGE

Fear Bréige / 149

GROUNDSWELL

The Apples / 157
Soft Rushes / 158
Dead of Night Love Poem / 160
Divination / 161
Scripture of the Wood / 162
Cloistered Man / 163
Golem / 164
Sweeping the Chimney / 165
The Burning Bush / 166
Cinéma Vérité / 167
Washerwoman's Lane / 169
Maquette / 170
Riviera / 172
Drowning Machine / 174
Lydia Jumped / 176
Belmont Mill / 177
Taken with Gooseberries / 178

The Night as in Her Hair / 179
Foundlings / 181
Daisy Cutters / 182
The Birdman of Nicaragua / 183
Amputations / 184
Red Deer Skull / 186
Scut / 187
Plastic Coal Sack / 189
Crow Conversations / 190
The Tunnel / 191
Brother / 192
Groundswell / 193
Imagining My Mother as a Sibyl / 194
Yeti / 196
Wetland Elegy / 197
An Afterlife for Animals / 198
Wind Chimes / 199
Divje Babe / 200
The Dead Petitioners / 201
Ireland's Eye / 202
Fastnet / 203
The House of the Fire / 206
Natural History / 207
Plague Bodies / 208
Soyer's Recipe / 209
At Pompeii / 211
Subterranean Song / 213
Seasons / 215
Song for a Centenarian / 216
Geezer / 218
Last Night a Starling / 220

NOTES / 224

for Judy, with Love

Introduction

Some poets make their way slowly, in fits and starts, to that place where emerging sensibility finds its own proper register in language. Others, luckier perhaps, are claimed by their own proper language from the start — and Patrick Deeley is one of those lucky ones. For him, language begins in the body, is shaped in his mouth by the body he owns as a boy and as a young man discovering himself, shouldering through trees and their undergrowth, stopping by streams, wading through marshes in the home place. It's the language of physical work, and of physical delight in his own unfolding mysterious strengths and physical perceptions. When Osip Mandelstam asks: "What shall I do with this body that has been given me/so much at one with me, so much my own?" he is asking a question that finds an echo in all of Deeley's work — the early poems are all about knowing and finding one's place in a world almost overwhelmingly present, the later poems more inflected by hard-won knowledge but always retaining that sense of wonder at the world. Not even Kavanagh has such a rooted awareness of the natural world, its textures, sounds, smells and silences trembling on the edge of speech. For Deeley, from his earliest beginnings, the world is that other place where we are most at home, including but not necessarily amenable to ambitious human presence, a place where sedge, rock, night owl, fox and band-saw hold their places as of right; the world is a place where each casual labourer or inarticulate-seeming neighbour knows as much of life and death as anyone else, and owns a language fit to express that understanding if we have the wit and tact, as Deeley does, to afford them the respect of unjudging attention. In the later poems, it is true that Deeley has learned to acknowledge and honour the wisdom gained in learning, and in the arc of his own soul-making he fuses the undying knowledge of the world directly and simply known with a learned wisdom of his own.

Nobody truly knows what it is that calls a poet to the craft, but in each individual case, if the work is achieved, we can sense where those roots go down, we can hazard a guess, perhaps more than a guess, at origins. It's clear in Deeley's case that being physically in the world, being deeply aware of himself as a sentient being in a world that is wholly generative and sentient in itself, is a major shaping force, a force, you might say, that "through the green fuse drives the flower" — except Deeley is no nature mystic, seeing the world as metaphor for some other, higher order of being. In this sense he is pure pagan, *paganus*, of the world and unswerving in his attention to this earth and himself in it, wholly content that the world should be no more nor less than the world. This energy drives him, but so, too, does his profound sense of communion with the living and the dead of his native place. This is articulate communion on both sides of the conversation: he draws his language from the language of family and neighbour, from "the parish of cagey linguistics", writes in the same syntax by means of which they inscribe themselves through work in the place they call home. When he writes that "the blood / perseveres in me", or when he finds in his writing hand the same weighing and measuring that a wall builder gives to a stone, this is an act of surrender to a common grammar of work, not so much a self-conscious gesture of respect as a simple acknowledgement that work is our common fate, no more and no less than what we do in this world.

His knowledge of craft comes constantly back to his respect for the hard-won knowledge of those who work in the callows and farmland of his origins, but his appreciation of its rewards and imperatives circles constantly around the carpentry and woodworking skills learned from his father, spinning out as far as Michelangelo's "hammer-and-chisel hands" in the white hills of

Tuscany. Against "the way the earth/swallows everything, how huge this process/and how unending..." ('Rocking Horse') he sets craft skill, and also the mystery and ordinariness of gift, so beautifully and tellingly invoked and honoured in 'Imagining My Mother As A Sibyl'. Technically, there are riffs on Hopkins in the backward stutter of consonant, the plunging sense that the pen, flying on the page, is trying to hold back the headlong rush towards expression — but like Hopkins, Deeley is too much the craftsman to let the poem run away with him.

He reminds me sometimes of early Hughes, the Hughes, say, of 'A Wind Flashes The Grass', where the mind that sees "The trees suddenly storm to a stop in a hush" sees also that it is necessary to move beyond description and inhabiting to the necessary human contribution, to the articulated perception that "the stirring of their twigs against the dark, travelling sky/Is the oracle of the earth." It is not enough to say what is seen and felt, it is also necessary to add human judgement, discernment, in all humility, to the sum of what is. In 'Scripture Of The Wood', for instance, where the poem tumbles from "screens flickering, sirens and lights" into a wood minutely examined, silently inhabited by bird and lichen, midges and ants — and by musket stocks, furnaces, "ships sailing the lost centuries" — Deeley drives on and through what has held his attention to: "...life happening/turn by turn of its deep dimensioned pages, hill and stream/vivified — fish, feather, fur and leaf surviving as/they did before ever I appeared, as they will do though I leave." This late poem of his rings backward through the work, back to "this place dreamed us all" in 'Dislocator', say, to "the losing and the laying claim" of 'Minding Goal', then echoes forward and upward through the poet's journey from that place to this.

That journey, I should say here, has been in the common world we all share as much as in that small multi-dimensioned parish that is the ground of the universe for Deeley. 'Fear Bréige', for instance, is a considerable achievement in taking stock of how our small battered Republic came to the sorry pass that is our present lot. 'Lydia Jumped' is unflinching, cuts straight to the cold heart, in its evocation of a life that ended itself in the gesture of suicide. There are other poems of clear-eyed knowledge and wisdom in this collection, but there are also adult love poems, poems of joy, words of gratitude for a companioned life. The final poem in the book, perhaps its major single achievement, 'Last Night A Starling' is a dense, evocative magisterial recasting of a life, at the heart of it a genuflection to his wife's sister art of painting (and indeed a genuflection, direct and heartfelt, to the painter herself.) Having cast his cold eye over his life and the world as he has known it so far, he ends on a characteristic note of confident modesty: "… And do these/suffice, that salve my needful senses so? Do they replace you?/Well, no."

Resolute, unillusioned, humble and definite, Deeley's unswerving attentiveness to the music of what happens is in some ways a considerable surprise in a time where knowingness trumps knowing, where concentration in the living moment is a lost art of silence. It is not, let me repeat, that he is some kind of rustic savant, bypassed by history, singing a world that is going if not gone; Deeley is a tough-minded man, travelled, savvy, humane and learned, as much at home in our common high and low cultures as any of his contemporaries are — and also, be it said, a considerable poet of the city. It comes down, I think, to a chosen emphasis, an elected fidelity to the world as it speaks through him — with his full, conscious, deliberate consent.

— Theo Dorgan
Dublin 2013

The Hidden Village

Languages

The sawmill blade blurs as it's speeded up. A burst of smoke
rises from the revved tractor's exhaust pipe.
I sit in the tin seat, watching the distended 8 of the leather belt
smoothly recycled between pulleys. You align
the ash log for splitting, then propel the rollered twin-plank
on which it rests forward, nearer, along. *Skirrr!*
Skaaarrmm! Sklllupp! The touch, the cleaving, uncaptureable
in any syllables of mine; the language of timber –
mute but legible tabulation of seasons fibrous in flow of grain,
in heart shake, spiral, twig knot – your concern.
I sit for hours, raising and lowering the tractor's voice.
It stutters or races, depending on what you ask the saw to do.
The whole village hears our industry's vocabulary.
Heads are shaking in benign disapproval: "O let them
at it; they'll get tired yet." And when we finally quit, the metal plate,
slowing to reveal its jagged teeth again, clicks
and tinkles as it cools, and through abyssal silence a ghost bell's
one long vowel tolls in our skulls. Carry the planks
indoors for stacking, tome after tome, on the workshop rafters.

Dry Stone Walls

If I make the same slow, methodical moves as my ancestors made,
it doesn't follow they'll approve me or amble
back. If their talk happens to be sunlight through the gaps,
there's still my lack of understanding that. As for
their hands, long converted to lichen and dust, these I may
less easily shake than shake off. Dry stone walls, their
only monuments, falling for years, are mine in the words
    I pick
to prop them up – by shape and texture and weight –
intending something to interlock. This is physical work,
though such a notion might cause the stone-lifters one and all
to laugh quietly beyond earshot. If I laugh in return,
I do so mindful that my bones are – after a fashion – their own.

The Bee Queen of Mullagh Beg

There was a droning, a stifled buzz, a tilt and a tingle.
We lifted for proof the armchair cushion – clumps of bees
and honey grids peeled and broke and spilled.
We met the woman on our way home. Dressed
all in black, which all the more accentuated her fair hair
in the late evening sunshine. And she was crying.
Or did we imagine meeting her, the bee queen
from a legend told at school or from a story that belonged
to Grandma Molly Headd? It scarcely mattered.
For in a world impressionable to fairytale, where nature
picked its moment to run away with us, her grief
might endure forever, our guilty conscience at having raided
the hive that prompted the armchair to teeter
on the brink of living in a musty Mullagh Beg hayshed.

Gallagh Man

Go 'way down that bog a dark spit below heather,
go sleán a fire for next winter. So I draw
the worn body out afresh, so I take its creaking limbs
to task, but little differ all my labours make
to Gallagh Man – he's skid-marking the floor
of an iron age, he's danced by the neck in a halter.
Yah, poor Gallagh Man, such a big softie
in his deerskin wrap I set to covering 'im up and then
again affording a peek, but oh the twist of rods
a strangler at his neck, oh the donkey hang
of his dangler – whatever harm he done, look
sideways on 'im, misfortunate still with stakes pinned
to keep his soul from flying, and the slept
flesh turns up here, cradling my open-handed entreaty.

Dislocator

Blue-black summer dusk hides the way to Sliabh Aughty's hills,
but here, blistered tar crimped into hard texts, foretells
a stone-bruise that awaits me still, a bumped toe
bound to bleed before I'm shod again for September and school.

I turn my back to Turane Cross, the proud petrol moon
of big Mex aloft on a crooked stem, the fresh pan-loaf smell
of Tony's shop where he fidgets and shakes
and can't get his hands to work the keyed-up till. Amn't I,

the Dislocator, lucky next to him? Twice put myself out
since April, twice the bone-setter's pushed me back in to mend.
Pain can win servants – go, come, go, tickle-itch
my healing – but re-run a wonder and it's lessened: with sympathy

slack, I'm off on a frake again. Shadows rag the ditches,
sudden start of strangeness there, no such thing as supernatural
unless yourself enthralled by your senses – or All
Souls' Night does a pooka's scald of piss really flither the briar?

O, O, O, pipe the cables, taking a short cut across
where the road bends, and transformer's the tall pitched pole
hoisting above me a portentous can, transformer's
the box conjuring behind curtains in Mrs. Broderick's kitchen

a tale of how the west is won. I want to laugh – Dislocator
doesn't know to cry – at the lost befuddlement
of *hungry sod*, the banshee's broken prophecy, and laugh again
the sad, sad seanchaí backing out from all ye

'lectrocuted ghosts, goodbye. Further it's the hurlers, milling
by the lamps of cars, sliotar's thud agin' a shin – mind
that leg but don't spare the timber, creases springing to my
   cheeks –
pull, Josie, pull, keep it on the carpet; and I plant myself

there, flexing for a swing who am declining instead
past the jagged grotto of blue Mary Virgin which two bats are
describing, past the deep-windowed, dim-big chapel,
tall stained glass crowning Patrick, Bridget, Jesus in his thorning.

The oak door never closes, and maybe Lena's
within, worrying her worn decades down to the last stone, maybe
Lodger Glynn – whom Teacher pronounces one of life's
true orphans – is up to his bedevilment, fumbling at the organ.

Out comes Fr. Doran, whose well-fed shiny head some consider
knowledgeable, who has 'the power', unspecified
but dangerous, whom Mikie Bryan swears is livened more
by racehorses and farm-talk than by notions of heaven. Salute him,

yes Father, Benediction, Sunday I'll be thuribling the incense,
but meantime on a stone two spiders are fencing
for a single silken string, and it's Mikie Bryan's contention
that Big Ned who owns the land doesn't own them, that none
   of us

owns – not me my all-American superhero comics
on which my bother is preying, not our sister the harmonica
containing sixteen reeds, though such cadence
she blows makes us feel she owns, not the Master his insults

nor Teacher the Lake District, not the lambs their short
runs, the bull his long horns – none of us owning what we use,
but now these path-stones chat about my feet,
and self-abandon's the message each moth wants to bring to light.

This place dreamed us all, path stones to the house, black stairs
of the cypresses inclined by breeze, spread, ascended
into blue dusk, into summer darkness, my turn now –
make the most, you'll be here only a while, dreaming all this place.

Big Ned's Guest

A man can't live on the wind – his bright opening remark.
I feed him stir-about after he proves unafraid of work.

Mucks out a byre or some such – oh, strong as an ox
in those days, less stooped, his head full of wiry red locks.

A man can't live forninst a bush. Untangling this,
I get him to shake out his pockets. A pipe and matches.

Satisfied he's safe, I bid him sleep in the galvanise hayshed
and leave him to it, certain he'll go the morning road.

It turns out to be true a man can't live in the way he says.
I work him fairly up until April or May, May it is,

then he absconds for the blackthorn breezes of summer.
Pipe and matches remain. And an ironic nickname. Lodger.

Lodger's High

Sunlight whiskers me cricked at the foot of a big leafy tree.
Road finds me out warping with hunger beyont Cappy Cross.
Lady of the house butters me a slice, dog begrudges this.
Grey cuileog shites, pulls a body-hair, wipes his bitty arse.
I rub an' I scratch, locate coinage in my tattered fork.
Night settles down, slugs a few stars from the noggin I sky.
Moon fills my mouth, I hail a game bush riding the ring-fort.
Last log ignorantly clicks to itself, thorny sparks fly.
Scraw of rumpety grass plumps slack up the size it should be.

Minding Goal

One upshot of being stuck between the netless posts
during hurling practice was the guarantee
at least of the task and satisfaction of hanging the sliotar out.
The others clashing and chasing, jerseyed
in various county colours, dreamed themselves glorious.
You squinted through oblique sunlight,
or pretended the shape of ease, or crouched, or paced,
depending. A save adorned the goal opposite,
and swiftly the game turned. Solo-specialist Joe
closed in, all wrist and speed as he balanced the sliotar
on his hurley before swivelling to lash it
past your ear. What kept you there? Hardly the prospect
of making a save. And retrieval was a long walk
no one else would take, a slash-search
through lank grass. Mullagh Beg, spring twilight, the losing
and the laying claim both implicit in a sphere
of corded leather tossed up before your face and given air.

Under Clonlahan Bridge

1
Your broken shadow cast, your light-headedness; and if water
once dreamed of only itself, the dream snagged
on something and there was life – cell so small, multiple
diffusion and gel, every organ, all appetite,
the great paddle, perfect dovetail of fish scales into a wetsuit.

2
A fish made to resemble a stone; a fish acting the maggot
in order to catch a fish; a side-on invisible fish;
a fish so intensely bejewelled it conjures a phantasm. Such
fish variously forever trying to fool each other,
to live by the tricks they play – yet none, you say, in this river.

3
Climb out of there before you catch your death. Climb stiff,
red-buttocked up off that rock, take silence
and the vast sky with you along, take the freckled sweetness
of a rainbow trout home to the pan; again be struck
by the notion that no one should ever miss us when we're gone.

Lena Alone

I was well off and didn't know it, my rheumatics quiet
for the summer, only the corncrake
keeping me awake nights. I always took a knock at the door
for insult. Just turn the handle, walk
straight in, bring me blessing. There was a key

you'd call communal – I never locked a door in my life.
Far as I saw, neither did anyone. Able
again, I cycled to Gurty, got the few groceries.
Butter vouchers filled my churn. I let the meadow,
kept a clocker hen. Church devotions

dusted my knee; I had right-of-way through darkness.
The late-callers wore mummer masks,
whooped a hullabaloo around me. I was lifted and shaken.
"Where's your stash?" My mattress gutted
with their knives, my dresser smashed. *"Where's

your stash?"* The sharp years flash across – I forget myself.
What am I now, looked at in the glass?
A wizened face, twitched by thin white stitches of scars.
It's falling dark. My key slots the lock. I hear
a reaper and binder working late, but no corncrake.

The Road Lorg

The tar road is anyone's, I'm below the head
of a blind boreen; the clay path's
for cattle, you can muck it just the same;
these prints aren't vixen's, here's where
the rabbit runs; step-up stile's
a good invention, Old John he does be leppin –
with a bucket of mash, a dash
of calf meal, days a splash of cold spring;
but the road beyond Mikie's
is so lonesome yourself loudens, the waste road
cutting a bog no one will burn,
the slippery road falling down along its sides
and the middle fit for joulting
a tongue-load of lozengers, my lumpy words …
Well, hold hard an' we'll see
do you know what you're at – I'm diving under
a low bridge's broken back, then
skiving over a winded log: this twist
of difference, this bruise finding correspondence
with images a poultice, this
tempo you can shake to, this hatband surprise,
and many a tumble yet to be taken
for setting myself up, for letting myself down,
and many a crooked turning
from the parish of cagey linguistics, the town
of dreary mathematics besides. Nor
should I go by the crow, illustrating the shortest
distance between two points as she flies.

Old John

Turf-heap and hay-pike aren't where he
dreams them, who could lilt just lately
sod's worth, saving behind each gabháil.
Now he's misplaced even the well,
misplaced it, Old John, and gone romancing
back seventy summers to the dancing
asterisk of a lit fuse, the sweating keg
of gelignite in a nook, the cold clear swig
come of such crack, water's plain truth –
arra himself, grown hollow with the drooth,
certain that some place a liquid coin
stares up – is tunnelled – long way down.

Cowdung

When 'watch out!' can't step you over or around,
but into it, just let the word *scuther* float.
Head this way again after rain has dabbled, breeze
and sunshine baked, after the brazen
yellow dung-fly's flown. There is scattered now
nature's good mould, slowly crumbling back
into clay. And – through the dung-spot –
greenest grasses imaginable, freshly begun to shoot.

A Man from Derrybrien

He had the shoulders of a horse, and the long face
of a horse, and the belly of a horse.
He clomped in his wet-concrete boots as might a horse.
He whinnied for a laugh. Threw the head
at this notion or that, flighty, suspicious as a horse.
Hired himself out in the name of a horse.
And shouted, if you were a mate of his: "Hello, horse."
Hauled a horse-load hour after hour,
and drank by night as became a thirsty horse.
Put his money on a losing horse. Shod
and groomed himself to make 'the odd gallop back across'.
Otherwise 'lived horse and got grass', cantering
memories of hills he'd never settle. Lost,
it took forty years, his wind and limb – a broken horse.
In Camden Town. Forgotten as a matter of course.

Sand Quarry Skull

We sat it on the tool-welted workbench,
turned it round and round, slow
cranial-dome world of caves and hillocks
a desert in our hands. But still,
but still, the skull reminded us of ourselves.
We dreamed ways by which a vessel
might fill, pour, be lipped, tasted,
known, might reciprocate or seem to,
might find the decency of a deep,
a lasting clay-break, when its time is done.

The Old Headstones

They lean. They sink down crumbling
round-shouldered. The very air
is eating them. Blithe colonies of lichen
nibble the fretted inscriptions,
but Mathias Hanrahan – whose last words
were an enquiry as to whether or if
the goose would be cooked,
Christmas Day, 1861 – and Sarah Kilcoyne –
mother of fourteen, stumbling
in famishment for a canister of flour
off the neighbours – dwell among us still,
dwell, are verifiable, beloved
morsels in the mouth of race memory.

The Pictures

The white protagonist pressed square-jawed
and zealous past mud huts where
the natives oozed admiration and bewilderment;
pressed fearless into jungle, speckled
distances ashiver with mire and python, feverish
drone of sun-fed creatures lapsing
into sudden silence – which a host of arrows
dispersed, loosed by savages stood
ebon and still behind trees! Luck contrived
to save him, his ambushers proving
in need of more stringent practice, even if close
shaves thudded impressively into wood.
He, armed only in righteousness, swung into
swashbuckling action, coolly dislodging
his enemies. And we, bunched in paint-flecked
musty seats, hoodwinked by his depiction
as hero, continued on supporting the villain.

Aughrim of the Slaughter

Though bits and pieces of battle can still be found, brass
or iron from musket or cannon ploughed up,
mostly nature spreads and deepens over everything. Thickens,
daubs, the way blood did then, blood in spurts
and squelches where the wounded lay with swords upright –

not in defiance any more but pleading to be put
out of their misery. And corpses everywhere scattered
were dragged about to serve as makeshift seats
or as beds beside the many fires the victors set near to night,
fires that eerily reddened the brow of Kilcommodan.

Local people assert they've seen the ghostly armies
materialise – as though each man's been spirited, at start
of battle, through a hole in time – and seen
through fire and smoke cannonballs flying across the gentle
dips and climbs. But these ghosts, if they could

speak, what would they say to notions of God or country,
to avarice of kings, to 'A la Memoire' and 'Died
on the Field of Honour' chiselled into a cross? Maybe say
the sentiments of peacetime or of our day are easy,
and wonder if we – pushed – would make a stand, in the cause

of liberty or land, on grassy Urraghry Hill or where furze
blooms round Attibrassil Bridge. No answer now,
no telling, and vanished the stratagems and counter-strokes
ordered by the Generals, quelled the cavalries
charging where Tristaun Stream and Melehan River are apt,

still, in simple misstep to take both man and beast
off-guard. Hushed the 'Bloody Hollow', where foot-soldiers
in their untold thousands fell, all of them turned to mud,
with only strands of rusted wire rambling the low,
lichen-spangled walls to care for what was so fiercely contested.

Friends

Me and PJ. PJ and me. Whichever way I put it
sounded good. Ran, raided, hurled, fought –
all one. Slugged the altar wine behind Fr. Doran's back.
Knocked the heads off tulips parading
along by Teacher's wall. Bathed in Keaveney's Well,
which half the village drew on for drinking.
Adventured. Until the May evening in Mullagh Beg
when a tinker lad stood on the sideline,
watching us hurlers train. "Get rid of 'im,"
our reffing mentor barked in my direction. I gaped
at the red-lidded watery eyes, the snotted sleeve,
the sawn-off wellingtons banding black
chafe-marks – *iroch* – across his spindly shanks,
and changed my mind. PJ said I was chicken – "Just
watch this." He waded in with hurley flailing,
battered that tinker lad down. "They're the same
as animals," he shrugged, when someone
chided him about doing the dirt. But I knew it would
never be PJ and me, me and PJ again. Not
that I was any better than him, merely the recognition
of my own soft spot, open to the world's hurt.

A Study in Juttings

Looking tonight at Gogol's old man in an overcoat
depicted by Yuri Norstein in flick-fade
animation, I see again Mikie Bryan, who dwells
across the Callows in his rambling house,
his black-thatch hovel draughty as bedamned.

It's late. The card-players have left him alone
with his drowsy crickets and a red hen that roosts
on his bed's back rail. The incessant wind
blows through to him as to Norstein's citizen.
And though no avid clerk meticulously scribing

what the world made office has done
or left undone, he is a conscience still, stirred
by beseechment of the dead and the living in a storm.
He untwines the day's newspapers,
neatly batched. Wrestles one, another open,

and leaning from the hob re-launders both flat.
His head tilts bird-quick, sizing up truth
in its various casts; his sudden finger stabs. A panicky
candle flame on the bare board before him
throws shadows that bounce, then momentarily

serene ascends to full height, cancelling shadows out.
Its perpetual poor light works the long
countenance to a study in juttings. He hesitates.
He asserts. Frets about Congo, Rhodesia,
giddily umpires the Space Race between 'Merica

and them Rooshians, damns down its own sorry hole
the mine at Tynagh that booms and drones
two miles over from his door. He says names
will change, map-lines shift whole tribes and tracts
of land. Says the human heart can be held

in a hand and still go on beating. The card-players
humour him, yet homeward below my window
I hear them scoff. "Rhodesia? Congo? He's some
pagan – he makes good poitín, though."
Misrepresentations might never end. He told me so.

1969

It was sunset and Claffey said: "God spare ye the health."
That's all he could muster by way of soothing
the burst blisters on our palms as we trudged out
his clanking gate, hay-dust's tickle at work in our throats
and the winnings of a hot-tempered day settling

in fields behind us. 'Jawbone hire' is all he would pay.
You shouldered the three pitchforks, home
a cross-country walk. Hairs finer than rakings wisped my belly,
my brother's chin. We declined the handsel
of two passing orchards, regarding ourselves as men.

A stranger, suited, self-assured, struck up with us
in the field known as Smoothing Iron. His chit-chat
primed some purpose we couldn't comprehend.
You stopped, looked him full in the face. "I was up north,"
he said. "On a job. You know what I mean."

Bramble-bush dark; stone stile. We were pushed on ahead.
Bits of talk followed. "Will you not do that
for us?" "Clear off to hell. You're talking to the wrong man."
You came over the stile alone, never afterwards
mentioned the incident. My brother and I grew away

to our own concerns. Two decades have elapsed, spillage
of taunt and threat, maiming and brokenness,
lives prematurely stopped. Over and back the arguments
run, the ends and means and grief of conflict.
I'm no wiser about that man, what he wanted, what he wants.

The Life and Times of Oliver J Martin MEP

1
Turane? No, I don't return half often enough. Now
Strasbourg, these desked documents, agendas and committees
keep me tick-tacking the emergent Europe.
A strong voice matters here. You could call me a huxter
or a horse-trader, a broker, a lobbyist, even a patchwork patriot.

2
Meanings need change only in terms of their magnitude –
well, that's as may be, for I still recall hock and fetlock days,
mouth of every nag deal pulled back to reveal
a gapped grin at October Fair. And the father beating down
Cheap Jack, so to gather me my first suit off the rack.

3
It was a start. I got into marquees, rose from the ranks
of wallflowers and shy countrymen, to entice among showbands
rolling off covers of sentimental songs. I caught
the jingle of spare shillings sifted in trousers anxious to get going
out on a good time, grease for the loins, a bit of a dance.

4
An open hand would slacken the grip of obdurate clergymen,
percentages promised to roof church and residential.
But what can't be overlooked is there was no place until I settled
into the shodding of a big ignorant field,
yoked up canvas, fly-by-night beading of bulbs to the six-pole.

5
Great entertainment happening outside and in, oh Ireland
swung for some while others started singing romance
couldn't swing her at all, but meanwhile I found myself coining.
Business diversifications, a sharp ear and eye
kept, a smiling mouth shut unless it was wise for it to be open.

6
Local issues matter hugely to people – parish-pump politics
is the term ye high and mighty media men call this
game I'm in, but street- or grassroots-level's where the plain citizen
scratches and scrubs himself, and I know about such
things, and I send a car to get the voter to the polling station.

7
Semblance beats real. If sincere is what you just can't feel,
lower your voice, wear sympathy's face, attain the effect of easing
the burden of the people's pain. Consider a funeral
good, a wedding special, a hurling match or a cattle mart adequate,
a crowded pub worth the expense in the year of an election.

8
Ireland – she always had more shout than clout – is a fecky
little bag of breezes, a bundle of odd arrangements, a glorified bird
sanctuary ... Ahem, Ireland is a great little country, famous
for her welcomes and with potential over and above the planning laws
and tax incentives, her empty beaches, her unspoilt sceneries ...

9
Oh yes, Strasbourg now, these desked documents ... Not home,
of course, not at all that class of beast, but tolerable.
And service still to be rendered. One of my residences sits above
Loughrea's speckled lake of legends. Come trout season,
I fully intend to push a boat out there with my German friends.

In the Boilerhouse

She moves her hand off a hot pipe
and laughs. The swish of divestments, his
follow hers, only standing-room

embraces, the spaces between whispers,
wait till I show you the place,
this is how lovin' is, my tender stranger,

we fire but once the breathy darkness,
touting health, pleasure, youth,
beauty – our bodies' ruses of invincibility.

Emigrant

Your train to exile, blunt-faced as a battering ram, moves
inexorably on its track towards the town's heart.
You see it coming from far back, past bleating, verdant fields
whose white-blossomed bushes shimmer
the mearings; past bungalows and barns built by cautious men
in a sudden spree of borrowed bank-notes, an optimism
that didn't last; past the straggling new estates
and the cramped 'tail lanes' where washing inhales the wind
and dogs swap rowdyisms. Suitcase in fist, you say
goodbye to loved ones, cry behind the consoling impression
of being 'lán dóchais' as Raftery. Your face
has the crag quality of dry stone walls, your complexion's
windswept raw, but in your accent run cadences
of softly falling rain. You proudly use the 'Bog English'
you were found guilty of at school, and which
some thought prudent to lose. And once on a faded wall-map
the Master's cane drifted off from Achill's finger
pointing west to "America, my lad, where you'll end up, soon
as you quit snagging spuds and turnips." Defying him
still, you go east, settling now to the iron clack,
reflecting quietly on Connacht's other tag, Cinderella
province, hurt that it seems so apt. Compartmented 'le ciúnas
gan chrá', her young take their naïve energy to hell
away, embodiments of Cromwell's curse gone wrong. A few
you recognise, migrants who faithfully return at weekends
to pick up their former lives beyond the limbo
of office and bedsit. Others, less familiar, boat-bound after
their brief Easter visit, earnestly do their party-piece,
men and women swaying together, beer-swill
and sentimental song gurgling in their throats for the oul' sod
of Erin that can't give them a living. You shake your head,

dismiss the pull of roots as fond-foolish in this
world-shrinking age. 'Be damned to it,' you say, the ghost pain
of amputation a debt you don't intend to pay,
while evening slowly darkens and compartment lights come on.

October

When I look again the Virginia creeper is sending
this pebble-dash gable up in cold
damp flames: so many turning colours I can't find
where one ends, a second begins,
or fully enumerate them other than to say October,
it's October already – and Magdalena,
the saying stills me, the act of looking dazes my eye.

The Chalk-Face

In memory of Conleth Ellis

It became a standing joke between us. You brought it in
at the end of each letter; I drew it down when we met.

It always made us smile in rueful recognition
of the classroom's demands. Beyond that, it was the dust

of time passing, the world's forgetfulness, things to be said
before the white shadow fell across our intentions.

I see you at the chalk-face, raising words to the riddle.
You have turned your back on life, but you address it still.

Ghost

The neighbourhood's appalled at the allocation of a house
to the ghost. Some people close their eyes,
pretend he doesn't exist. Others dredge up old accusations
about chains jangling, scrap being thrown
around the place. They say he doesn't keep himself
well, deny this is the stain of their prejudice
showing through his whiteness. They resent his irregular
lifestyle, the way he vanishes into his former existence
only to materialise again, making a mockery –
they say – of walls and, by extension, of all solid meanings.
He wants to know why walls can't be there
to serve him rather than he them, puts his disappearances
down to business and the pull that's always
possessed him since first the tribe was interfered with by spells.
Gone on his summer rambles when hotheads
burn his house to the ground, appalling the neighbourhood
in the glare that follows into saying
the right things. Now he's ditched – the Council
'making every effort' to reallocate him – under bushes
turned winter-bare. You can hear in passing
huddled children haunt the dark with their cries and sneezing.

The Crucifixion of Tommy Joe

Tommy Joe, telling himself, telling us, he's 'sartin-sure'
his ewes will lamb, his weanlings fatten,
his barley ripen, 'in the gather-up of three seasons'.

Tommy Joe, dancing out and back in his big buff coat,
who 'never bothered at all with the women',
whose house might be empty without him, so.

Tommy Joe, aged fifty-nine, owing a pound to no one
and himself not being owed, moochingly
loosening a button to piss on the frosty road.

Tommy Joe, digesting the Tribune of a Thursday, the quiet
pint nightly, faithfully 'follying the hurlers
though they wouldn't puck shite off a door'.

Tommy Joe, climbing the gate to his yard undiscouraged
when foot slips, chain-wrapped top spar
snags, flinging him headlong over, one ankle wedged.

Tommy Joe, losing his hat to the ice-mud
just under his head, cursing, struggling, pleading his last
at a world all gone from the way God made.

Tommy Joe, poor crucified, whom morning will find
limp on the gate-web of iron, his buff coat's
unfurled linings resembling a giant moth's flithered wings.

Tommy Joe, his back turned to all he owned –
shocking us the news there's no telling what can happen
when bleddy blind circumstance is not your friend.

Panache

Even your labours decline you in their redundancy.
Who will scythe a meadow
as you did, or pitch hay, or press
a breast-sleán into a sodden turf-bank today?

Nobody. And nobody is sorry.
The long-handled back-breakers you lived by
hang from wall-laths, rusting.
Your haggard's a weed-embroidered museum.

Yet if I could compose poetry
the way you shook barley – those seed-pellet
syllables, that old battered bucket
a headful of shifting nuance – my lines would swerve

and hop, I'd cast the words
precisely, with panache, my hand opening a blessing
to the winds I'd know were coming,
that they might not lodge but let me sway.

Axe

Not deep, this digging of a space for a bus shelter,
no big rupture, the effect of an eggshell
breaking under the drill, shards of footpath, soft
subsoil, pebbles and grit. You find resemblances –
a rib, a femur, a skull – bits and pieces

you suspect won't remember us after we are done
with waiting, with articulating heaven
as a sunny day, a win at the races, a lover's kiss.
Cars whizz the N6, everything looking easy-peasy,
the slick, mesmeric roll of Esker Riada

west to Galway, east to Dublin, so all-fired seamless.
But what's left is the stone axe the last man
dropped who knows how many centuries ago, maybe
on a grub-break or by his children or his
enemy called away – take it, natural as a handshake.

Marigold

Lorg is far away as ever, but look at me, a man
still embarked on vagary, stooped
to the panning stream for a flick, a gleam
of minnow. Grass-bank bounce,
the harvest frog happens now. Withering sedge
and marigold in water are reamed
by skit beetles. My stocktaking fingers trace
a washboard brow, my wet kneel
creaks its cold. I rise to go, no more
the hop, skip and jump that propelled me once,
rather a measured pace, longhand's
earned headway over heart-stitch and mirage.

Crank of Nature

Mikie storing up his bones along the lag weeks,
edge to edge of winter solstice,
in dreams may breathe on a lens, a lens, a lens
of the Edwin Hubble telescope.
Oatmeal and a gulp of water from the galvanise pail
keep his marrow making, there's
blood-sustenance in a raw egg, but seldom at all
he'll stir out unless to pooley or piss
under the crab apple ditch. And what will
newspapers be but passing glances, the world a fable
he concocts, who by crank of nature
sits up till Tibb's Eve eleven moons of the year,
burning candle wax. So let them
who are connected to the electric juice hobnob,
bloom beyond this striped bolster his head
barely dents, this pulled blind, this topcoat over him.

His First Word

for Alan

He stomps round the room, lisping his first word,
light, as two syllables. I applaud him
and the word he's in love with, then turn again
to the story of Leonid Teljatnikov,
power-station fire chief, curtailing his vacation
when told about Chernobyl,
voluntarily entering the hell-mouth
which would breathe on him
for three hours as he fought to keep
the reactor roof from caving in. He recalls Tisschura,
Vashchuk, others who fell.
Now he awaits death, or a miracle,
while here my tired-limbed child tugs impatiently
at my elbow, bringing me back
to the light. Soon I will carry him up
to restorative darkness, the still-possible good night.

King of the Wood

Rathgar Pastoral

Half a century or more ago, a Rathgar woman
kept a cow, which she stabled nightly
on ground we now call garden. What was then
open country is all but inner suburb; swallowed, too,
the calp quarry and its over-spilling lake.

A lone windmill, deployed to drain the lake,
whirls again in a story told at bedtime
to set our children dreaming. The quarry cow
slips our minds. She wanders off to graze the spaces
between strewn boulders, where grass glistens.

The woman is unconcerned. She ambles into
the setting sun, just away from our sapling
Victoria plum, which is opening in blossom. Casually
as my mother might, she reaches for
her milking bucket and starts to rattle its handle.

Monkey-Puzzle

Again we find ourselves carried away by the thought
of having discovered each other. And in
your garden now this monkey-puzzle, fossil mother
of suburbia, suggests South America.
Wild, we both say, in the parlance of today
or yesterday. Except it all started ages ago – the way
we talked to beat the band, the love play
we wanted to make before the diplodocus that peeped
shyly round a tree could be taken for a common
streetlamp, the blundering brontosaurus
trembling hedge and tarmac become – in a heartbeat
or a time-slip – our last bus back, the one
we might run to catch or contrive to miss on purpose.

Instrument

It could function both as pen-holder and paperweight,
this raft of tubes moulded together
and glazed smooth to the touch. Mostly
I let it idle. But once, looking out at the green swirl
of a tree tousled by summer squall,
freshly budded leaves plucked and tossed, I thought of how
the goat god pestered the nymph
with his amorous attentions – she escaped
literally into the ground, to emerge again a reed – and then
this came to me as mouthable in a way
that words are not, as something I might blow
through to eloquence beyond words,
until even the tune itself must fade, stilling ode and elegy.

The Mantle

Scant sloe bush and shellacking hailstones
saw him off, who shouted
hay and oats for the Mullagh goats,
eggs and rashers for the Corbally slashers
along these country roads
where he found no welcome in any house.

And maybe he was the last
of the wandering bards, forgotten except for
the few scraps of his rhyme
that took the ear of my mother's mother –
she in her hushed fashion
would later wear the mantle of ballad-maker,

composing verses for her son, the village
blacksmith, for her friends
in Castlenancy, for the young boy who saw
a prayer-book floating in a pond
one Easter Sunday and tried to retrieve it,
imagining that he, too, could float.

But when Felix Doran lived among the people
of Killoran, he played and played
and played *Toss the Feathers,*
The Jolly Tinker, My Love is in America –
and, early or late, nobody grew tired
bar my grandfather, who farmed and farmed

and farmed, and tried to wean Felix
off the pipes, out to flock sheep or milk a cow.
It happens over in my mind – fun
and music emanating 'as good as sunshine'
from the house of those 'prime
articles' the McColgs, warm-hearted laugh

of my mother breaking the spell
even of her own unavoidable absence as she
recalls snazzily dressed Felix
waving from a muddy headland his furious,
immaculate cuffs. Life's slow
diminuendo might make me sentimental

in my turn as I gather under the plain mantle
those who wore it before me –
Molly and Tom, Mary, Sis … Sad Hynes
tramping head low the road to Gortnagappa,
who seldom spoke. 'Georgie'
of the bushy beard shuddering from us

in a flounce of rags and a woebegone cackle.
And gently as makes no difference
gather from the pond the small
drowned angel, while the ghost piper
plays us out by haw ditch and windswept hill,
crying the world though he's bound

to laugh it still, laugh it back –
even as we may once more be found to laugh
in the mouths of those who follow –
laugh the world back, through his inimitable
'bubble and squeak', to where
hesitantly but inexorably spring is breaking.

Wood Rap

for Genevieve

ASH

Girth of grace, last leafer,
spring back, black-nailed finger,
hurl on the ditch, loam dreamer,
stay later, sappy splayer,
smooth skin of green silver.

PINE

Braille bod, text of cone,
shrewd shedder, green porcupine,
make a stake, take a tan,
ramrod, resiner, rangy man,
tree of tar and turpentine.

OAK

Twist the air, broad-bowered,
father of names, royal lowered,
acher on, depend on jay bird,
slow grower, bog's word,
home to species highly numbered.

Hornets' Nest

A paper lampshade, but many times layered, at the tip
of whose warm, plump cone no bulb peeps,
only a small black aperture designed for entry and exit.
The flat base is glued, not hung, above our heads,
in the boilerhouse. Summer gave us no reason
to potter here. Now we're too late to see the hornets.
But taking heart from wonders which the world,
if it ever stops to think about them at all, might call
insignificant – earthworms gowned in a froth
of mating, earwigs hatching and nestling their young,
or those grasshoppers we met in a Wicklow glen,
hosts unwary enough to let us touch off them – we cherish
the elaborate, empty nest, the notion of a lampshade
wrought from regurgitated bark, flowers, sap;
we envision nature as living lights that range forever out.

Burren

If I quicken here at all, I stumble; if I stand still,
glares and glints of reflected sunlight
make the white rocks appear to alter and move.

My walkabout dreams up a bubbling puddle
to enthuse the turlough, dissipates
tepid water through rockery cups – earth, vessel

of vessels, turns tipsy on scents of wildflower,
is cracked about the clutchings of tiny, ancient trees
growing horizontally in grikes below my feet.

The Antique King

1
He is lowliest of the underwood, making food
as Sulphur Tuft does, sparsely, from old tree-stump
and fallen log that has decayed. He worships
below the picture, keeps one eye on the cathedral crux

of branch and bole. He suffers shade,
suffers cold, feels the slow upturn and spiral into leaf.
He gathers gnarl, draws on dapple, sounds
and renders the wood afresh to itself as his own word.

2
Let me follow his rolling realm, dream those gentle
hills and villages he paced before the first
rumblings of the wheel were heard – a strict pastoral,
where good repute depends on word of growth.

The people make demands – his magic
responds, pushing the sun up, the sappy stalk, the crops.
Let me catch his laugh, now, while the hale
and credulous world lollops under his spreading hands.

3
He will be cautioned by whispers of the withering
of canopies even while verdure still
covers him as a cloak. Of a day turned out to shiver
next the shorn, winter-blasted trees, he will learn

at his leisure that magic's a falderal,
and power a fluent draining of the god by his mortal
body, and pride disposable. So, laid low,
he must huddle, become another endangered species.

4
And when I fail – as he fails – my poem deemed
unworthy of its tree, then may you shake
your head at 'nature's fool' with his nose still sniffing
the spring wood, his ear pressed close

against a summer-swept bole, his eyelid batting at
a fruit-clustered twig, and declare him profoundly mad
for showering such a squall of untenable
language loose: the blossom, the leaf, and windfall.

Sub-fossil Tree Shore

Incongruous, of course, to find trees with their roots in the sea,
but then these are dead and branchless
whom only the barnacles take to and the salt sprays foliate.
Soft soap ebb slop slides among them;
the clay-stinting rocks won't grow them back. If I press
for metaphor, they leave me slack. And if
my mind goes worrying the lost woods of Connemara and Clare,
I'm still slipped by pine-stump remnants
of primeval forest all buttoned and coated with bladder-wrack.

Impatiens

The Busy Lizzie Thomas brought in
would never amount to much,
its soft stems broken at the elbows,
but such was the ceremony
with which he presented it, I made room
among the conkers, cones, acorns.
Soon we returned to the graft
of sums and spellings. A box of chalks
had worn out before either of us
again thought to remark on *Impatiens*.
(My composure had withered
in face of the riddle his mind posed.
Thwarted by abacus but not coin.
Spelling *sing* for *sign*, yet an able tracker
of fox and rabbit.) And the plant
had proved me wrong. All branchy now,
a leafy spill down the cracked
plastic pot. Come spring, it blossomed,
pale pink asterisks, and Thomas
decided it might be better off in his caravan.
He, too, had gone before June,
head shaking: "You see, I served
my time. I've roads, not books, to travel."

Fruit Man

Plums in thick beads weigh the tree down,
causing branches to shear and peel
while yet attached by the merest slip of skin.
He fondles the ripe clusters – packed
almost conical – dandles them on his palm,
brushes lightly where the tree holds cold

though the sun shines. Each plum
is purple, but with glimmers of red, pink,
gold, pale green. He shakes the bole,
and little clicks come through the leafy rustle.
Suddenly, with surprising thumps,
the plums bounce; a few shrivelled leaves

spiral on their slow descent. Vigorously
he shakes. A black and yellow wasp
whirls in close circles buzzing as if to shave
his scalp. He brings his hands up,
windmills furiously until the wasp flies off.
His hands touch his face. Nose, lips, chin,

he pats and presses them. They don't feel
as the plums feel. They feel papery,
coarse, and they seem not to fit. He stoops,
noticing a solitary plum has fallen
into his basket. The rest lie scattered
at the tree's foot, or peep from tufts of grass.

Some are bruised, their skin broken, their
jellied innards showing. He shrugs.
There are far too many to eat. A punnet
or two for friends, the rest will
rot, soften and spawn a grey fur of mould,
adhere to the bowls that contain them.

Finally he'll dig a hole in rockery clay
and empty them in. And forget about plums
until white blossoms dress the bough
again, bringing him – in the lift
of a new spring – devotional as the legendary
fruit man of the Moluccas tip-toeing

round a clove tree to whisper and dance.
But this one plum sitting in his basket
bothers him by its difference. Lopsided; dark
brown battling other colours out.
He picks it up, revolves it slowly between
fingers – dry and scaly in its unlovely

skin where an insect nipped, all the succulent
energy spoilt, no bouquet when he
puts it to his nose and no ease in rolling it
along the rigid red line of his lips
or about his overly rounded chin, rather a frail
scraping that causes him to wince. His eyes

cloud. He can't see the scattered plums
or the plum tree any more. He hears
the mournful sound of the wasp returning.
His fingers bunch. The rough plum
bursts. His fingers rid themselves of plum-flesh
until there remains only the moist,

wrinkled stone – it is here, just as he's
set to toss it from him, that the swarthy wasp
lands. Stilled to fascination, he watches
the rapacious insect dip and pirouette, probing
for those last vinegary vestiges,
then hears it gnaw to small avail, and trembles

remembering how the young man
mumbled 'we was only havin' a lark', and how
the judge decreed a suspended sentence.
A jam-jar of acid splashed in his face as he
slowly cycled home, a daylight moon
following, diaphanous, with just one cloud,

February's cold air cuffing his ear,
the weathered nests of a flown year creaking,
seeming to sail amid rigging of branches
black and bare, no bother or niggle for he knew
that his wife would see through
palaver about bird's-nests and moon, yet cover

with ardour – it was Valentine's Day –
his absence of flowers, would wait for him
at the door. He flinches at the tingle becoming
scald, opening blood and bone, skin
and flesh flapping loose, gristle being eaten –
his frantic hands, his mad fingers

seemed to stick to his face; the young man
and his grey-hooded accomplices
ran; for all he knows they still run, honking
and whooping their ecstatic laugh.
The wasp, how curious it is, taking stock of his
unsteady hand. And the tree, gathering

yearly to a gallant harvest, yet such a scrawny
wretch of a thing planted that bad winter
when reconstructive surgery's slow
graft began – paroxysms of anger and shame,
half-remembered scraps of himself
dawning in the patchwork face in the mirror.

Strangers glance, turn swiftly from him.
Mouths of friends move, overcompensating
with talk. She kisses him on the mouth
though his lower lip caves and there is merely
numbness. They manage a getaway
together. Heat burdening his shoulders,

narrow hilly streets, at evening the cool
consolation of her fingers winkling him, slack
muscle and skin's ticklish undertakings.
Germanic hymns drone endlessly
from the old church overlooking their hotel.
Incongruent, for this is a haven of

honeyed light and red clay swirling in thick
rambunctious rivulets each time
cloudburst happens – brief, explosive, always
at sunset. And the women stroll
barefoot, carrying their sandals through deluge.
One merciful night a bolt of lightning

puts the hymns to bed and he and she find
something to do with the silence
and the dark and the spring of desire begun
to muddle through. There's the tail-end
of that heat here, gift and continuance
of an Indian summer – he idles, dreaming

her kisses anew, her concupiscence
a gentle pucker of lips gone testing and teasing,
tongue touching tongue until love
grows fierce and all's to make, all's to mend,
their two bodies drawing down among
squashed plums on the stained earth strewn.

Nature and our Devices

By the base of the river wall moss grows lime-green,
fluorescent, dwindling as it rises out of damp.
Towards the top of the wall, graffiti run riot – names
and dates and arrowed hearts. About mid-wall,
moss and graffiti meet – so discreetly this could pass
unnoticed, as when ivy appears to reanimate
the telegraph pole it's spent its whole life climbing.
Or picture a tree come to cover a streetlamp
with leaves, a green-tinted shine filtered through these.
Well, if nature and our devices are at odds still,
notions of symbiosis don't seem altogether absurd.
For leaning here looking down I could swear
the graffiti's converted to moss, the moss is made word.

The Addergoole Cot

Since it went eventually down to dream
among my townlands of Addergoole
and Lurgan, I must stop and suppose a great-
great-grandfather's great-grandfather

felling and hollowing Ireland's hugest oak,
fashioning a crude canoe, a communal rowboat:
fog-breaths of ferried cattle occlude
its every twist, cargoes of lumber and chat

draw close to home. The lank-boned
paddlers come, each with my thin face, my own
and my father's hawk-nose. Calmly
they size me up; their teeth whet old saws

familiar to my childhood: "Always work
the dry hour. Turn only the bright side out."
While this cot, their craft, so long sunk
in obsolescence and so well preserved, floats

and flexes them all in favours passing for more
than figment or silhouette. No answer
can I make before they again go, adrift
in reeds, aground in bog clay, their legend

a buried artifact full of forgotten rudiments,
their endeavour expended unavailingly
even if the river still wends its way, the blood
perseveres in me. And I am sternly alone,

telling myself their calluses have turned
to snail-shells, their ribs wrestle blackthorns
round by Lurgan and Addergoole, their
shrunken skulls are mushrooms springing still.

To the Dryad

These woods were first the seat of sylvan powers,
Of nymphs and fawns, and savage-men who took
Their birth from the trunks of trees and stubborn oak.
– Virgil: Aeneid (Book VIII)

Beseechments of winter lift. Not as cloud and not as my tilt
at these perennial ivy-clusters sporting on high
their black berries and top-heavy tangle. But lift in the way
the tree strikes me differently – as airings
of your shimmy up where branches leaf themselves afresh,
elbowing, occluding the world I know. My climb
is less a far-fetched fancy than the need to sit loose-legged
amid your canopy, crowned by sun, holding
the imprimatur of a clear sky in my hand. Below,
the villagers move by earthly weights and measures, certifying
with seed and fertilizer how and why their gardens grow.
I call by names they pleased to call you long ago:
dryad, green-blood, god. They ask if you tap your head,
or smile sideways, or show yourself to the newly awaking tree.
But what throws me – and has them fall silent
now – is the burst of a dove from your branches thunderously.

For a Gardener

Then I stood acquainted with the Lady Chapel
hid in the side of St Joseph's,
and caught the silence tumbling in splinters
of stained-glass light from two windows painted
by Harry Clarke. My eye fell full
on 'Our Lady Queen of Heaven in Glory'.
Not the form alone, more the colours emanating –
green, gold, lemon, blue – all among
the Biblical women, all a bower I would bring
alive here, spade by hour, my climbing
season come, my benchmark clay, sun and shower.

Yard Sticks

Stepping the felled tree was a balancing act
I often tried in ash woods of childhood. Branches
gave trampolines. Or where they jutted
stoutly upward, climbing poles. And when the bole
began to roller, I leaped. But each tree
implied furniture. Lopped of its limbs, trailered
to the mill, it became planks and yard sticks.
If I twigged to aesthetics of leaf or bird,
or to the gap in morning a downed tree makes,
there they still were – yard sticks – stacked
for the carpenter's apprentice. Slide rule, set square,
found my measure. But when, one day,
I unshelved a pencil from behind my ear, its scribble
caught the whisper of blood and imagery
flowing together, slowly decoding *samara*, the keys.

King of the Wood

Winter egg-breakfasts. We saved the shells to helmet twigs
of spring – which was a whitethorn tree, buttered
and creamed with primroses from the ditches, and danced
    around.
Our childhood, if we but knew, a wilding dolled up
in pagan ritual, a throaty echo of the barbarian's lost hurrah.
He threw shapes with us there, our woodman father,
stubble on his chin and sawdust in his hair. His old credulousness
from before the calendared moon, the unreliable sun
configurated to clock, had been gradually tempered to a gentle
wisdom. He became tranquil as the summer wood,
his speech so many silver-grey ash-trunks ascending to leaf-
    canopies
of interlinking branches. In his face, the sun's luminosity
was occluded now, now a sparring opulence. Once,
he lifted a hand to shield my eyes, and it grew green-blooded.

Woodman

Not second sight so much as the eyes of deep experience
enabled my father to see through to the heart of trees.
He discerned the ringed grain, coopage of winters, summers

contained, and understood how it would run in terms
of the flat plank, the curved contours of the hurley stick.
He could tell how many hurleys per tree, and was alert

to the knot's mischief, the bind of broken growth. Tree-sap
would come into his eyes, he'd see a way to seasoning.
And yet, his considerations of timber as a crop,

so much grist for the sawmill, planing in the workshop, were
tempered with appreciation of the tree as aesthetic.
The beauty of its four displays, its composure under duress

of the sun's pull and earth's, made him regret his task
more than once. At Ballydoogan he stroked the silver-green
trunk of an outsize ash, cleared his throat to speak,

stayed silent. Necessity squeezed all his options into one in that
ferocious contest between chainsaw and wood, where
arm-strength coalesced with steadiness of nerve, where table

and chairs were made and hunger broken as food
through dint of hardship turned to good. Sentiment, then,
was akin to a toadstool squashed at the tree's foot.

And he satisfied himself he was leaving at least a dozen trees
for each tree he felled. The years of his apprenticeship
sprouted afresh at Woodlawn as dusk silenced work, bottles

of Guinness throttled, his memory's miles to Duniry
cycled back, pittances recounted, a shilling, a pack of *Gold Flake*
at the end of the week, an awkward job in the offing

always – felloes for cartwheels, joinery of furniture, use
of chisel and auger, a farmer planting a spade, stump-handled
on the bench-top: "Whatever else, don't burn out

them bleddy rivets." Laughter softened everything before
he realised he was encountering these or similar tasks,
more than forty years later, on days when he worked at home.

There, spectacles perched on the hump of his nose, hair
and eyebrows flecked with dust, he'd pass for a contemplative.
Was it the shaping, his arms framing a diamond space,

shortening and elongating in their to-fro concurrence
with the plane, brought patience as he leaned in at the workbench
salted with his sweat? Or was it the way ends met?

The penciled delineation of a pattern along a plank,
his solitary superimposition. He'd proceed from this guideline
to carve out a freedom for the hurley asleep in ash,

with such clarity of vision that, textured and unique as any
hand-wrought thing, it would sing its praises and –
by way of consequence – his own, on fields of furthest Sunday.

At night, hunched till late, wedging myself into the white spaces
between the lines, I'd hear him pronounce my fate.
And maybe words *will* be the end of me yet, nothing transmuted,

the page still as it was, pulped straw, rags and wood, the man
still uncelebrated. Dublin offered a roomier space,
heyday and high noon, my own mode of expression. The woods

were mentioned by letter now, casual remarks about 'lots'
and 'stands' and 'cubic feet', 'foresters' and 'fellings' and 'old
    estates'
dispatched to my new address, the wistful light of boyhood

leaf-filtered, ever at a slant. "Stay at this job long enough
and it'll kill you," he said. He decided to follow his body's advice
and retire, allowing for one last wood. Careful cuttings,

sizings up. His final tree falling against another required a high,
angled lop. The prophesy he had made came bitterly true
as he took one small step back, yet far from here, and forever.

Red Sash

Wearing plaid, wearing short, heavy-duty jackets
and steel-caulked boots – train-wreckers,
corduroy-pavers, revvers of chainsaws, wisecracking
descendants of the Red Sash. I saw them
in a film, wintering under bark. I heard tell
from your brother who'd been to Northern California
and back. (I'd not gone when he asked.)

Our sawmill tested me, and I the lumberjack myth –
in local Galway woods. The blade's
haranguing journey through each ash opened a gap
in my beliefs. And after you had died,
'at stump', as they might say, I thought of how the film
grew quiet, of how they untied a dead
companion's boots to hang by the laces from a tree

standing nearest. Makeshift commemoration, I suppose,
the best that rough and ready lives could manage,
but this gesture I kept clear of timber
because you were my father still and for always – smiling,
unbroken, on the go – in memories borne
beyond the pitiless incidentals of a chipped
fingernail, a foxglove sprouting at your temple.

Sap Myth

The Basoga tribesman on TV
knelt and sipped from the axe-cut
which he had sunk in a tree.

Was it respect, or an old
curiosity concerning the taste,
dipped his head, I wondered,

or a humour of his forefathers
honoured. He never uttered a word,
the move was swiftly made,

the camera momentarily eluded.
A commentator interpreted
this mouthing of sap to signify

brotherhood – tree man, man tree –
but afterwards in local
Ballydoogan woods I sank an axe

and felt the story come to me
purely and simply as a cure
for thirst. Bittersweet, intimate,

though I cannot say a green
god's blood had claimed my tongue
only to free it. Nor say –

even if my most tender lyric grow
from a tree – that sap I drank
in childhood gave the air to me.

Dargle Oak

A forgotten thermos flask, stuck under the oxter
of the tumbled oak. Which is itself
all but forgotten, the god fallen, with one intact arm
jutting out of this hillside. Rummage
below the mossy coverlet; mouldy bark and tuft
of wood come to hand. A white grub
with an orange-capped head plays dead. And here,
a sheltered surprise, ghost of a green
chance – oak-leaf sprig-god, redemptive, yet to rise.

Pollarded Beech

I still call you queen, though you lost your head
years ago to a forester who turned
firewood squire, cropping off the bough.
He so forced you to bear the absence of true branches
that you must squat and swell,
holding the gists of grand leafy lofts
down to make solid as dead heartwood, as gnarl.
Yet no containment's possible.
You fiercely attempt the old crowning grace, you sprout
at weird angles, in rods and shoots,
frazzles and tangles, in splinters
almost, but for the mending glove of your skin.
I still call you regal, overlooking
your grotesques – a wood-knitted
owl's face, and a rat's – with fractal calculations of leaf
and limb, with manifold twists
coalesced in an aerial pool where you catch the sun.

In Killalaghton Graveyard

Only scraps of the old stories stay, yet sufficient to show
how full of enchantments nature stood, long ago.
One woman saw the bare stick which she had leaned on
in hardship blossom with a change of luck.
Another envisioned a tree branching from her own neck,
and the dream foretold that she would found
a dynasty. Whether by saint or pagan moved, the earth
bequeathed good. Or, having its favourites fall,
the earth bedevilled. With Patrick's religion winning
a fervent multitude, tenacious snag-sinewed
older gods clung beneath the whirr of blessing and miracle.
It took famine to loosen that grip. The woebegone,
thinly crying towards heaven, ate clay, pushed clay away
in their dying into the now-despised ground.
A story still is told – of a woman and her daughter,
who came hoping for respite from the hunger,
and died here at Killalaghton. This ash tree is said to mark
their grave, its roots bedded in the clayed forms,
turning every last vestige into itself. Glancing afresh, we see
it's far too young. And dismiss the folktale.
And yet find ourselves sparing a thought, because the tree
occurs to us now as a prayer, by seasons green
against each death, or cold and bare, staying serenely put.

Names Remain

Even the hard-headed landlords could come up
with a poetic turn, proclaiming trees
'the feathers of the scape', yet next breath prepared
to pluck them as 'an excrescence of nature
for the payment of debts'. Or as 'a shelter for all
ill-disposed'. Names remain – Aharlogh,
Dromfynine, Glanmore, Glanflesk, Glangarrif,
Glanrought, Leanmore, Kilmore, Muskryquirke,
Kilhuggy, Glenglas, Glenconkeyn – names
that dip and sway, creak and sough, beckoning us back,
somehow, to the broadleaf groves, the last
wildwoods, through syllables which hold their music
still, though they are twisted out of the original.

The King of South Galway

Ask and I gave. That was my weakness,
a refusal to refuse. That was my strength
in the beginning. Hat, topcoat,
veritable shirt off my back. And as I gave –
ewe, cow, horse – word went
wildfire: criticisms, esteems. Neither
did me good. Who would be sainted alive
and stay level? Who would be
classed a glory hound by some, by others
plain mad, and keep his cool?
I walked the shores of this big lake, this bulge
in the Shannon, and cried to nature
for solace, for avarice even, for the stints
and generosities by which
my neighbours live. I might as well have been
a kingfisher nesting in the rib of a river.
Or an otter ruddering – fluid's
own incarnate – to whom the gods permit
no alternative. "Your eyes,"
said the sly man who had come from
a long way off, smiling, sniffing out the legend –
"give me your eyes." And I twisted
against these fingers glutching the round
gristled pain of it all. Down demented here
to wash I go. The lake wells up
about me, reddening – 'his wound's reflection,'
people say, and their Gaelic clears it
as *Dearg*, Lough Derg, the sight I gave away.

The Dissatisfied Youth

I keep to instructions. Choose a wand
from the willow, whittle it down
to a quadrangular figure and place it over
the lintel of my parents' door.
The house remains dead. Long faces
stare, bodies sit unbudgeable.
No conversation and no kick from anyone,
no leeway given, nothing mooted
that's new or different or for fun.
The only moves are mine – a whirl of angers,
stomps, gesticulations – all my steps
mislaid by the dance-maker's tune.
I throw the willow figure back, its surfaces
scored with the exact runic spells
he gave. I declare him fake, demand
a refund. But he replies there's
no compassing these mysteries.
They misfire, being whimsical, otherworldly,
of trees, and we yet learn something.
That it's high time for me to leave.

Son of Hazel

Finnéigeas tells him the sources of the seven great rivers
are wells, and that nine hazel trees overlook these –
the nine trees of knowledge. He describes
how the hazelnuts shake free, singly, intermittently,
through the good graces of so many sunbeams, raindrops
and ripening winds. "Each makes a little plop,"
he says, "surprising the quiet places; each moves
on mystic bubbles, inspiring even the fishes." Finnéigeas,
old poet, vows to catch one such hazelnut
if he is spared the eye. The youngster takes him
with a grain of salt. Mimics his mincing steps as he comes
and goes. Stoops to tediously mesh and mend
his own fishing nets, to treat them with birch-dye preservative.
Whistles until the day a hazelnut is gulped
by a salmon – which carries the knowledge on to where
Finnéigeas hauls it from the Boyne. Then
whistles again. Is thrown to tend the smoking stippler
on a spit. Sees a blister rising. Impulsively
thumbs it. Jabs his burning thumb into his mouth –
and suddenly the super power is fired in him.
Mac Cuil, Son of Hazel, the disgruntled but forgiving old poet
names him. And he, whom the storytellers
will put – through dint of linguistic gusto and derring-do –
to alleviating the dark nights that were lived
back then, sees, because he is his own man now, the future
clearing, all atom and essence slip within his ken,
all his untrammeled heart's impossible saga of harnessings.

Críochán Thorn

Was it three or four blackthorns he had uprooted, the man who
could muster neither arm nor leg when he
tried to rise next morning from his bed? And what became
the character found darting between two bushes,
unable to decide which he should fell first? If the folk mind's
a landscape, you stand *mounded*, Críochán Thorn
of the Slieve Blooms, bidding me keep my distance. And I do,
but with a mumbled word or two, a little
mocking gesture made about your crookedness. For I know
the shape of malevolence was never yours, just a scare
you threw across the moonlight, just a shadow
grafted to the thoughts of people fumbling for a way that might
leave them unmolested. And if the ruse has helped
to protect you, keep it, keep it so. But tell me about the man
   who …

Cromlach's Deception

That my fingers and toes, the leaves and lobes
of my leprous ears, my tongue and nose,
might grow pristine again, again be whistling clean,
I wash in the Shannon. Little good its splash,

and less ease. Then the sainted relics
from Europe strike me as curative – I quietly
bundle them into the hollow elm at Clonmacnoise,
and wait up for morning. The abbot

would surely smirk, pronounce me vain. I say
bad cess to him. But come dawn, all I know is pain.
The elm withholds my potential salve.
It has swallowed and sealed everything. I take

an axe to it. But where the axe strikes, woodchips
fly back into place. And when I kneel
to sever with the buckling cross-cut, sawdust
again turns whole. I'm bested by a pagan miracle.

Baile and Aillinn

He was coming south to court her; she, making north
to meet him, when the false words
of a stranger – who visited one, then the other, back
and forth lamenting "Your love
is dead, your love is dead" – broke their credulous hearts
and coldly accomplished what he said.

A yew tree shaded Baile's grave; an apple tree
dappled Aillinn's. Here the story might have ended,
with his face arboreally remembered
and hers transmogrifying branches. Except that the poets
of Ulster decided to carve the yew
into a tablet for their verses, while the Leinster poets

similarly ear-marked the apple bole.
At Tara, Cormac Mac Airt presided over the poetry slam.
He set the tablets side by side before him
with kingly tact. Fabulously there they leaped together –
wood grains, metaphors, calligraphies
all twining and fusing in an apotheosis of the love act.

Ash

Whether your title is 'Excelsior Fraximus' or 'Venus
of the Woods', you were once the Big Bell
of Borrisokane, whose branches no one dared burn,
in thrall to a legend that they'd fire the house.
At Kells, you genuflected above St. Keenan's Well,
and promptly bled – a miracle more palatable
than the idea of red-rotted vegetation in the minds
of the multitude. At Killura, made sacred
to Craebhnat, you were rent and rendered, your bark
and twigs, your shavings stripped by emigrants
on their way to the ships – a charm against
drowning, if not starvation – until eventually no trace
of you lingered. But let the scholars glossing
your name and fame lay claim to the tree they know;
you dwell among us simply as ash, you raise
from the plain gifts intended for our silence, our eyes.

The Flowing Bones

Dandelions

The longest yields a three-foot root. The shortest
squeaks a snaggy tail. Sod and spade,
where would I be going? Not out with the diners

tonight. The bouquet of restaurant
will have to do, breeze-borne from four doors down.
And this lawn, lit with dandelions.

Their stalks break bitter milk on my skin;
they give nothing unless they give
everything – the withheld scrap comes up in clusters.

And I, levering them through mats of grass
with meticulous gentleness, lull myself into believing
I loved them in an earlier time.

There seemed to be room then, abundance
of wildflower places, but these were weeds still –
they brought me to my knees, I cursed

tillage, the big darkness fell, the world wheeled by,
suiting itself until I forgot and was
forgotten, and grew alone, and knew this was natural.

Callows Water Barrel

The goldfish turns silver, then black, enlarges
with the passing years to make a legend.
The tadpole destined to stay forever limbless
extends until the length of your hand.
The minnow, briefly glimpsed, seems ample
as a trout. Child, you seek for what
can't be proved by trawling a butterfly net. Your
imagination runs deeper, and deeper yet.
Through the murky bottom of a Callows
water barrel, past spits of mud and grit, under
the subterranean river shilly-shallying
between Mullagh Beg and Keaveney's Well.
Until you become the world's fool hereabouts –
far gone by nature into the mire, with
dwelling loneliness your dreamed-up behemoth.

One of a Kind

Then this tough vegetative tangle,
couchant under the weight
of altitude, is stumbled on
in a valley in the Andes – by a man
who suspects that what

he's found is one of a kind,
and plucks a sample. Laboratory
analysis reveals a fossil tree
propagating itself, each
stubborn step, each fix and twist

in the colonising sprawl
an encapsulation of centuries.
If not quite immortal, surely
a Methuselah lives at large, a wonder
of the wilderness. Maybe

yet to find itself, after a makeover,
at home in gardens where still
the dream of a waterfall or wood,
a plant or animal surviving
undiscovered, comes to replenish

an outback in our minds,
to wend us towards a secret held
beyond the mountains,
plumbed oceans, found and fumbled
world caught in our map's net.

Keaveney's Well

Didn't ask who Keaveney was,
just took everything off – shoes, clothes,
sunhat – just took yourself
away from sweat and haymaking,
slid between low walls. It
might have been a stone coffin,
one of those ancient cists,
possessions arrayed about you
except that here the cold
submergence burned – senses said
you hadn't lived before this
steeping of your bones. Clay
and marl juices seeped;
cress, pond lily tickled; the one-minded
school of minnow turned.
Land aspired to be water;
water wanted to be land.
A trembling happened, a bubble
spun glistening, then the great
taboo tail of the subterranean river rose;
you dreamed the evening women
come to dunk their pails.

The Marl Excavations

The dankest imaginable smell comes up
when you pull a flaggard, shank
and root, out of the soft spongy moot
where the Callows river meanders
to a standstill. Black earth smell,
but not that of the bog, which is civil
by comparison. No, you inhale
now a great conglomeration – rust
ooze, insect oil, fetid vegetation,
drowned horse, sheep, heifer, diluted
droppings of the long-gone crake,
plover, Greenland goose and gander.
Yet you must lean down further in,
squeeze pottage of fibrous soil
between your fingers, hold it close
to your nostrils. Because it alerts you
to the hare's-form squat of childhood,
the marl excavations: white, with
small tell-tale shells remembering a lake
where the Callows found its first
foothold – and where your heart's
pangs are shallow waves, breaking still.

Wellspring

One more story coming out of the earth sees this
slimed creature hauled onto a flagstone,
sludge in his boots and hair. There's a stone-bruise
at his navel and he smells, as the rope
untied from his waist, of gravel. All day he has hacked
the grime loose, sent it by the bucket-load
up through the whirling, dripping air, who now
is the last one looking down. Below,
the gouged chamber sits, its floor leaking bubbles
in the darkness, and gurgles, and chill rivulets
cleanly trickling. Though he doesn't say so
yet, this well will draw a village to haul its water home.
It will see out drought and deluge. It will
be the measure against which he sets city fountain
and burst main. Stooping under pretext
of tying a shoelace, he will study the dimples made
by raindrops on a pavement puddle, he will
address the scars of a passing breeze, and feel himself
begin to compose – the weathered day,
the settlement of mud, the well envisioned, swollen
to its brim. His grey reflection will be cast in.
He will straighten as if still wearing these stone clothes.

Territory

Ben Bán, even Poppyhill, will be tall enough
to feature in the finished picture. As will
everything. Climb prepared to remain
until cloud and hazes clear. Detail the sweep
from Scalp to Inis Mór – tree lines,
waterways, dry stone walls, coasts that seem
hardly other than notional. Haul up
the theodolite of steep and undulant images.
With nightfall, let the limelight be on fox
or badger answering to your stillness.
What matter if all was better said and done
before? Now you are leased the wonder
of fitting grey-eyed Lough Rea in, of gritting
beside it the statue to Stoney Brennan,
hanged for stealing a turnip. Leased the city
of teeming tribes, technology's wavering
landscape, lane and fieldname slipped, ring-fort
turned roundabout. Leased the puzzle
of where Shannon's Callows begin and end,
whose the dent on a cannonball found
at Aughrim, what the mother word for Kilrickle.

A Burrishoole Gate

All the days we pass through, it swings from where
its two sections of rickety timber
are tied with twine at the centre, swings in the wind

that blusters full against our faces. We
call it 'wind gate'. It makes no sense because it marks
no point of exit or entry, and adjoins no fence

other than a ditch we'd as surely cross
with half the hindrance. Below and above and about it
nature happens too hugely for any containment.

The run of laughing rivulets, the shifting mist
in cahoots with the bare heads of the hills,
the rainbow spanning a lake – these powers beyond

the powers of reckon and render that would have us
quarry a mountain down, or bulldoze
a wilderness to accommodate a rubbish dump,

seem now the subtle setting of the world
to rights: we watch them come and go, fade and flourish,
free in the open country round a Burrishoole gate.

Muslin

The island woman came ashore on a bigger island,
settled away from the sea. Her Gaelic dried
in her throat for want of answering. Her lore
was shrugged off by the new people. She held to
her shawl. And when the local children
bundled in, she sent them to the shops on small
errands. Unwinding – it always seemed
to take an age, and it always stilled them – her pennies
from a measure of muslin she could trail
to a ship the sea had washed up, sixty years before.

Frogs

No barrel of laughs, hoisting
a broken-backed bridge
out of the stream
with grapnel and crowbar,
with bare hands.

All's discolouring sludge,
marl you must plunge
down into. Until a sudden
jumble of frogs.
They've sat through winter,

cold customers
still blazoned with harvest's
golden overcoat,
still fat. Dandle them
on your shovel, cast them up

to exterior grass.
Everything lies in wait,
mower and drought,
beak of bird, the fox's snout;
everything's to suffer

yet, even the dead season
springing a frosty tail.
These must leap far, carry far
the world they contain
entire. Softly cast them off.

Capstone

This garden wall is cherished by more than me alone.
The roses and the apple branches rising
out of its grimy foot stand sheltered, while the sun,
taking all day to come round the houses, lingers

in every crevice, every mossy spot. At evening, a game
of bluff is played between two magpies
and a feral cat. And when darkness falls, woodlice
climb to graze damp pastures of peeling whitewash.

The wall's crumbling, pocked and blotched. Here,
my gritted elbows sit. Here a crown of ivy
was blown off. And here, dream-garden possibilities
present themselves – foliated, trained and trellised

along fancy brickwork. Still I keep to a bargain struck
with the rain and the powdering frosts –
a wall stands, there is fervour even in a forgetful head,
something held sacred under this slipping capstone.

The Cailleach

On the shore at Beara, the caileach
finally comes a cropper,
dashes into and fuses with a stone.

Or so the myth tells. It's implied
that she started out beautiful,
desirable, obedient, good – the words

are interchangeable. In the course
of the myth she develops
a taste for sorcery, dissension,

herbs and potions injurious to what
the pharmacists of the day
might sell. Domestic duties

fly out the door; she grows slovenly
and wild. Warts accrue about
her nose; she sports the gossip's

big chin. A saint wanders
into the picture, or maybe a bishop.
She takes a shine to his

magic stick made of Bog of Allen oak.
He chases her to the shore
at Beara, the summary petrifaction.

If the myth's laughable now,
with the cailleach seeming to flourish
as she pleases, there is still

a woman can tell how hard and for
how long she herself – in
the manner of her mother before her

and her mother's mother – has
had to bang her head against the stone,
to wear it down, make it open.

Birdsong

Perspectives through sound: a blackbird's
oath, sworn from a chimney-stack;
the mellifluous coos of woodpigeons
conjuring sunbeams amid high ivy clusters;
a robin's pipe, happening to approve
of cotoneaster berries. But if the tremulous,
piercing notes of the thrush
are expansions of space and time, rolling me
wide and far, I still hear the magpie's
screeched assertion from a wall overlooking
the covered-in quarry, that all was
winter yesterday, was stone the day before.

Cave Life

If limestone asserts the sea
once stood taller than this inland hill,
it still only begins to shape
the twisting tale. There is never

simply nothing further – we go
through squeezes, down.
Sunless for a million years, creatures
can have no use of colour.

Slowly the long dark quenches
their eyes, skin finds ways
to redefine itself and them. Bat radar
switches on, and the snake's

knack of tracking heat. Antennae
extend, frail yet fitted
to tap the twists of crevice and crystal.
Change hazards everything,

and we are not immune. Heads
swelling in our acceleration
of knowledge and pride render us
the more prone to topple.

But that here we stop, humbled under
wonder-wheels of calcite fruits
and flowers, of beast and angel shapes
with all the time in the world

at their disposal; here we dream
our first emergence from the rock, our
bald skulls smooth stalagmites
spanked by exploding water drops.

Species

I might find them subsisting still
in soggy Callows, on the sides
of ditches, in old graveyards – those
herbs, wildflowers, grasses
that put the first spring in my step;
I might pluck their names from
an almanac: vetch, bird's-foot
trefoil, orchid, summer snowflake.
Then to inhale the smells, be
dizzied again, bear with grace what
rash or hay fever was on offer.
I might even bring myself to touch
the last, exquisitely dappled
boggle-eyed caterpillar, set a ripple
running through it, shout my father
back from the brink of ecological
disaster, lead him by his grainy
fertilizer hand to stoop with me there,
over wonders of cuckoo spit,
spider and cowslip, on a headland.

Piecework

Mushrooms could become their own lamps,
flickering on and off, though I never
discovered whether this was a mechanism

of spore-dispersal or of self-defence –
I simply picked them, threaded a tráithnín
through the pedestal of each in turn,

and carried my bundle home. Sheep pasture,
damp autumn, mushrooms would
spring up overnight. Bog-English was

the only language spoken. We'd be
turnip-snaggers all our lives, the master said.
He had us measured for the sleán

and shovel.
              Boys and girls of my childhood,
I try to map your exile now, I strain
my ear to catch your altered accents. And

perhaps you in your idle moments
return to a misty morning picking mushrooms
in our Callows, a free-range life before

travel found altogether new meanings. Or
maybe you'd as soon forget this land
forced to sump and mulch, its wet meadows

drained, its people shifting out from
back field to main road, its menial undercoat
hidden, the long tunnels where the Polish

and Latvian women move, pale-skinned
in semi-darkness, pushing through piecework
with their baskets of button mushrooms.

The Last Seanchaí

His laugh comes from below the belly,
below the groin, and his laugh
shakes him all the way up. He slaps
his thighs to help the laugh
along, he tickles his sides. His laugh's

a familiar animal in our rambling house,
or rather several animals
which he keeps contained while the story
opens, townland to townland,
Carrowshanbally far as Eskerboy.

Between the lighting of his pipe
and the first spit in the fire, events take
a delicious or a drastic turn.
These spellbound faces, our parents
young again, these lame old men

redrawn to vigour, these holy women
gone funny in serious places –
what are we to make of them? Nothing,
now his tale's at an end,
and we listen past the punch line

for a hoarse lock turning in his throat,
a rusty wheeze as of gates
opening, before the pent-up beasts
of merriment burst forth,
neigh and bray, squeal and howl, and all

our lesser beasts of laughter
lift, gambol among them — this must be
the resuscitation of winter earth,
this the perpetual moonshine
where play the dead, this the hearth-song

we will scarcely recognise
as having belonged to us, after he is made
to exit blinking from the sight
of the TV in the corner, with his
'God save all here' stopped on his tongue.

Night

I looked up the kitchen chimney.
An echo chamber floating
amid soot tempted me to shout,
but then my father's snores

came trembling down the stairs.
Night was otherwise hushed
huge, full of potency that forbade.
Old-men jackdaws roosted.

The old-jackdaw men had tapped
their pipes empty, departed
with a spit. Their stories fingered
my spine, so many chill tingles.

I saw one framed star, faint and far
from meaning in the black
heavens as my own constrained life
amid the dying ashes. What

had the stories intended? Something
I might live to discover –
that the fort field, the Callows tree,
everywhere I had made free,

was haunted. That water and wind
and light played on the world
in ways I'd be foolish to upset. That,
for all this, life was open-ended.

Simulation

The red squirrels take off away from you
across the grass, towards the trees,
whose trunks they will climb –
always in scuttling, roundhouse runs.

The ducks stop grazing and scatter
at your approach, becoming airborne,
splashing down where the pond's
widest. But if you cause disturbances,

you settle at the same time
everything back in what you consider
its natural element. And receive
the bonus of close-ups: a furry face,

a frittered acorn, a loose feather
gone dithering airily onto another level.
There, a swan sails in apparent
serenity past her inelegant offspring,

to hiss in your face, to raise
a bone-breaker wing. It's a video game,
of course, and if the red squirrels
are pushed out by your introduction

of the greys, if the mallards fail
to identify poisons you've set for rats,
if the swans happen to asphyxiate
on synthetics or bottle-tops, you can

always revert to the beginning. So the red
squirrels take off away from you
across the grass – towards
the trees, whose trunks they will climb.

Mistletoe

A bird wipes its beak on a branch of oak,
or dribbles its droppings there.
Unwittingly a seed is set. This requires
sap's nurture. It plugs itself
into tree-power. The arrangement's sealed

with a disc. Out of which mistletoe
twists – evergreen, antlered. Now
we're swayed to the mood of the disgruntled
primitive, glancing about for evidence
of a bud. Now his joy is ours

as we discern the leafy wonder surviving still
in a winter-bare wood. Should we
call it 'all healer', or 'gift from the sky god'?
Or take such ceremonial pains
as the oak-man took to counter grief,

raise a blade and nick the elevated parasite
into a white handkerchief?
The notion's absurd. Yet despite these
head-gears and thinking caps appointing nature
to our will, we suffer as the maker

of the wild medicines suffered. Who still put
the mistletoe up, old *kissing bundle*
among the festive lights, and in a lull between
song and chat come to countenance
ourselves as sprigs of spirit born vulnerable.

Rocking Horse

My rocking habit comes from the horse
my father made me as a child.
Wooden, unpainted, and now that my children
have caught me rocking to and fro
to the *Bucks of Oranmore*, played on the radio,
those uillean pipes such yelping pups
and *Miss McCloud's Reel* altogether uncool,
I've half a mind to tell them of that
beloved horse somewhere turned to sawdust,
of how the sawdust slowly blackened
into earth, untraceable the way the earth
swallows everything, how huge this process
and how unending, how it will
encompass us all, such is the earth's rhythm.
But I stay shut. So it is my children,
young and well-disposed towards the turning
of world in their direction, who suffer me
and the ancient grace notes flitting
about my head their nods of sympathy tonight.

The Owl

Not that you are able to leap the fence
any more, but that you are able to imagine
leaping it. And the faces of your
long-dead parents appear to you still,
'blooming' as when they were less than half
through life. As for the owl you'll
never catch again, remember how you once
caught it, in the bog of Killoran,
to which you'd come footing turf, shortly
after your wedding. And make a play,
with down-turned hands, with supple wrists,
for my father before he was my father,
dancing about you his wonder dance.
Imagine the owl, ghost even to itself, in a bag
swung gently home. The same owl
that in your telling flows up the chimney –
gone, with all that seemed for keeps,
into thin air, yet yours now dispassionately.

Bluebell

The factories were here even then,
the pylons fizzed above this same stretch
of sad canal. Juggernauts creamed
the asphalt hill. And sky might
be raddled with sunrise, or clouded grey,
but was traversed, either way,
with cables which I'm still in the habit
of counting, thirty years later,
from the vantage of a push-bike,
below the brow of Bluebell. Imagining
blackberry rambles, a country village
away on its own, with woods
enough to coax shade-loving flowers,
bluebells so profusely pooled
a child might pick one for a place-name,
and everybody else agree to wear it
afterwards. But all I can attest to
are the pylons and factories – and this
piebald horse, standing glum,
his paddock a patch of cutaway ground.
Once, I dreamed him the original
inhabitant, old man of the place,
the king dispossessed. It was a myth
to shorten my journey. But again today
it comes around, as a startling sound
assails me up by Bluebell hill:
the trouble-boast of a rooster, flung
from a hollow heaped full of tyres
and junk metal. There, with flames
blazoned on his breast, he raises himself,
rattles his wattles in defiance

of our convoyed progress. And for
a moment I credit the earth is breaking
at my heels afresh, as a horse,
a rooster, a capercaillie – all fabulous,
indefatigable creatures restored.
And that the child has picked the bluebell.

Millennium

The mill of traffic unhinges. Bleep and glare
dwindle to silence and to grey.
We take in the high broken window
through which birds loop, the chimney sprouting
a sycamore tree. Our Thomas Street's
slovenly ancient: 'pound' shops
hold; steaming Guinness stacks; all that runs
to ruin's illumined by fine art
students and Harry Clarke! While yet
a big yellow crane lifts something gone bust—
the old tailor's bereft, and won't be back.
Further, Robert Emmet is hanged,
drawn and quartered, in a heroin fix
outside St. Catherine's. But Digital Hub, how
are you? And cobble lane, greened
by down-flow—no wild cascade, just a slick
of wetness sliming some citizen's
shed, his wall and bed, since before whenever.

Journey

The cement factory complex stands taller
than this drumlin we've begun to crest.
From a mile off, the black lettering on its
forehead frowns at our approach,
its unwieldy stack of compartments appears
through trick of the mist to lurch
across the valley towards us – as if a juggernaut
of the east, unswerving and unstoppable,
or a local monster from a local lough,
had taken umbrage. But enlightenment
as soon breaks on our minds,
burning superstition out, clearing swamps
of their legends. And we are certain
no secret's held beyond explication
even in the well that resounds with what seem
to be human cries, or in the thicket
where a wraith is said to shiver and levitate.
Now the saint of old, stepping
onto a stone and surfing it across the Shannon,
might look at us and be gob-smacked.
Now the serpent determined to avenge
its other half – one more road-kill
in our modern transformation of the myth –
might plunge its head in vain against
the flank of the chariot we are embarked on.
So the ripple of apprehension passes –
a primordial reflex – just as the hulking shape
of the factory itself dwindles into distance.
We anticipate air-conditioning
and power showers, plasma screens presenting
impossible feats, incredible sagas
before us in a hotel at the end of the motorway.

Dust

Then the world placed in my path
Common Earth Ball Fungus,
the thing so much a semblance
of our old football – leathery skin
flaked and tattered because left
out in all weathers – that I
simply had to kick it. The cloud
of spores unleashed a desert
about my eyes and ears and head,
and I found myself, drought's
demented preacher, prophesying
to high heaven that dust would be
continuing, dust would never
die, there was no cure but raise
dust, let dust inform, dust inspire us.

The Badger on Orwell Bridge

might have in mind to haul between his forepaws
these parked cars, maul them into one
cacophonous rending rejoinder to the traffic
that outside him flows. Except he's gentle.
So instead he must fall in love with the slick pelt
of the road, which he samples briefly,
dangerously, with his nose. He's come up from
an older world, past the luminous tag-art
adorning the under-bridge, come lumbering
through the tubercular slur on his name,
the last-ditch stronghold, the blood-sprayed dogs
of his baiting in a field where we stood
dumbfounded in childhood. And though
we fret for him all over again, maybe he is safer
settled here – the city's shyest customer,
unwittingly rekindling the matter of our own
animal nature. Which permits the lopsided moon
its astonished place in the pageant, swung
beyond the chimneypots and the flickering neon;
sends us following the white willows down
to dwell on the river's garnish of sensual green.

Fisherman

He seems to have set his gaze
on night descending above the Dodder wall
against which he is leaning.

There is nothing, his whole demeanour
says, need fuss him either side,
road or river, not even the rod

which he will almost as a gesture of homage
lift, once in a while, towards
the white willow holding the far bank.

Again he'll cast, always without looking,
in token acknowledgement, perhaps,
of the breeze or a heron's

silent passing. He can't be taken
as fishing for anything. He is all disinterest.
The cigarette dangling from his lip

has some time ago gone out. When
a moth plops into the water,
its belly-flop breaking the silver skin, he

hasn't heard, he will not look.
Then a flicker of trout, a splash of high tail.
He doesn't know, being lost,

apparently, in currents of lamplight
or in his own flow. And just as not much of
anything makes you want to watch

any further, he's turned into the sudden
tugging on his hand and eye,
who now, without to do, will land the fish.

The Bear

Pigmentation on cave walls,
a man thinking
to capture an animal,
or maybe to capture an animal's
way of thinking.

And in my parish a man
who could cajole
a bull, another who'd whisper
obedience to even
the most high-spirited horse.

Neither man would tell
his gift. I began to credit
the state of animal
integrity or natured separateness
could be waltzed across.

Except that this bear, he
of the delirious smile
and the murk-coloured fur,
was nobody's dancing companion.
He'd draw his own plans

up out of the ground,
where something had made
the mistake of moving,
or pluck the air down,
a sumptuous banner of smells

invisibly streaming,
and bundle it in wads about him.
What odds a berry bush
evading his juggle,
a salmon his slap, a shellfish

adrift in the sand
his lock-picking hook?
Or, if I was safe in bed, dreaming
myself a bear, this
hand become a bear's grip?

The Roadside Crosses

One pierces a grassy verge
which otherwise looks innocuous,
shined with summer's gloss.

A second slants against
a wall of speckled dry stone
swaying around a bend.

A third is sunken near the sill
of a white-washed gable
where a red geranium burns.

I count thirty seven crosses
in all – thin, sunlit,
fringed with black polythene –

thirty seven crosses troubling
the brief, lovely miles
from Aughrim to Cappataggle

with memory and warning.
A local protest. Death-sites,
approximate pinpoints

for grief not mine but pitched
along this road I take
by heart, who now might ask

if my neighbours offend only
their own elegy, or if
misfortune is all the road's fault.

Except that I am brought
back by gable sill, by speckled
stone and patch of grass,

to cognisance of the stranger
who smiled and dreamed
and was expected elsewhere,

who never once imagined
carnage would claim him here,
and in whose bloody wake

my hands must gentle
the dear, dying head, my lips
tender the contrite prayer.

Tuscan Afternoon

The birds of Montecatini come to hand
under a restaurant canopy
to pinch my bread. Not facile in their flight,
but struggling up against the air,
against their own weight
and nature, and then as if to hell with fear,
they land, snatch, are gone.
Through centuries this little theft
has happened over, no love or kinship, no hint
of sainthood implicit, no muse
making fresh, only hunger's whet –
still today the scrape of feather and claw
tingles my fingers, shoots
along my arm. I exit to stone pelicans
elevating fountains, architecture
of eagles flanking outsize gods and fated heroes.
Is it these keep stealing a march
on the moment, these or the dizzying heat
or the cicadas droning
through the evergreens? Now Michelangelo's
hammer-and-chisel hands cut marble
in the white hills, Alighieri
peers through his death-mask dolefully back
at Florence, Ghiberti's bald head
sits amid the Biblical engravings on the Gates
of Paradise, while across
from the baptistery two men go gesticulating
down a laneway – Ghiberti himself,
and Brunelleschi, old rivals found flesh again,
flying at each other as they
argue whether this dome, that tower, all
the thronging art of Tuscany will stand or fall.

Foxhall Sunset

Gaps in the whitethorns admit me to this
once and once only sunset.
Mikie, your shoes are growing weeds
in the haggard; I saw your ghost
trying to slip them on last night,
trying terribly until the moon
gave out – those shoes stood rooted.

Lena, your mottled hand
will touch your beloved chimney-breast
in vain; the only warmth
rises from the flank of an animal –
your cottage is long converted to a stable.

And maybe it's appropriate, John,
that nettles claim your proud
angry heart, for what kindness could?
But listen, I'll tell nobody,
the woman who came closest
set her love letters to you under a stone,
where they have slowly withered.

Where else did the importance go,
the immortals telling stories
while I hid by a gable, hearing and seeing
and never uttering a syllable?
Old neighbours, you should be
straightening now, shielding your eyes

against the sunbeams, with no
moral to draw from ditch or dry stone,
no talk of tomorrow inherent

in crimson, curlew-shaped clouds,
no other day, just this darkening landscape
where your houses sit a while
and the trees of your childhood
keep their appointments with the crows.

Bare Branches

Arms, knuckles, nibs – poised on air –
scribble invisible signatures.
A skeletal tree, a bleak aesthetic. If I stare

long enough, the tree turns familial,
ancestral even, and I am tracing there
bloodlines, maps of kin. How they

confluence in my hands! Seamstresses
dressed in pinafore, haymaking
women, ropers of water from the well,

ballad women yeasting solid ghosts
to rise us out of work and rain. Must they
so soon go? And with them, tall

baggy-trousered men – my grandsires
of proverb – who wielded axe
and wedge, worked cross-cut, delved

in revs among pine and ash with disc-saw
and ancient tractor? I'm listening
still. The hurley turns, shaped and shone;

they warn that life's a process
designed to knock my rough edges off.
And here – I hold with it a while –

is nature's word that not last summer's
leaves alone, but every summer's,
are commemorated in the bare branches.

Le Gave

About us the Pyrenees, thronged with trees.
Le Gave, by what springs and waterfalls
did we reach this level? To lean
over a rock and fathom the feeling of falling,
to raise our eyes and imagine we soar.

Grasshoppers click amid the melting snow;
butterflies sunbathe; stone breaks
into flower. We invoke the poet Russell,
who scaled these mountains, sang these caves;
we set the eagle of legend dropping

a fish on the besieged castle at Lourdes.
And it's a case of step in, be taken
at the ankles by the cold waters of Le Gave.
It's grey matter, part of the background
that isn't noticed until it starts to run – then

you recall the brown lizard of Lora del Rio,
which climbed to become the town
clock's confounding hand, and I the green
lizard of Ballydoogan, whose livewire
tail once broke off to write me a red scribble.

Mars

It stays with us, a red splintering of the blackthorns,
as down through the hills of Derrybrien
we go. Below Duniry, in full glare of our lights,
a rabbit falls prey to a fox. There's a pool of darkness
on the road, and this carcass slung over
the fox's shoulder is the same creature we saw
earlier, grazing the pelt of fox as grass.
Fragranced air, jizz of leaf, earth's life-force, belligerence
in blood, contention between creature
and creature. Until, hours later, home to a home
away from home, we witness the yew tree,
ancient and terrible, seeking fresh root amid concrete,
in a regenerative circle of its dipping branches.
Will it mourn for us, who dream ourselves the mother
and father of the house, at our withering
wave a waxen fan of notice? Light-headed, weary
with travel, we envision a future familiar in everything
but that new people will supplant us,
interpose themselves as we do – just as we do now –
at the exact holding point in the constant
sundering between what is ended and what has begun.

Ghosts

Of course they exist, taking such forms as might leave us
all the outdoors for doubt. Pass themselves off
as the heron standing among shadows in crepuscular water,
the bat skimming your flicked-back tress, the owl
patenting my figment of flying saucer. Songsters now, they
speak garbled languages, trills, ululations that open
to our every guess, floating bodiless above these woods
and conurbations. Even at stroke of midnight
they act up, or set the wind rushing ahead of us where
birch trees huddle white-legged beside the tumbling Dodder.
Strange, they make us think not at all morbidly
about the dying ground into which we soon must sleep,
our worries done, but rather would have us marvel
at this dream that raises the owl, the bat, the heron, the wind
and the song. Ghosts. The reason why we venture.
The haunted story of two lovers living here their lucky hour.

Fear Bréige

Fear Bréige

He got away from a field of barley in County Galway,
wood-bones wearing trousers and topcoat
and wide-brimmed hat, hung casually a few squally days
by a roadside, nothing occurring to him,
straw stuffed up his sleeve, a pair of black eye-patches

fastened across his rag-bag face. Labourers trucking back
to the city gave him a lift – paraded variously
around the building site as 'boss', 'commis chef', 'rare
tulip', 'night nurse'. Cue a spew of jokes
and uncouth guff, but whoever would harshly judge them

mightn't as quickly grudge them the standing room
cleaved under their lime-bleached boots,
the 'floats' of gargling concrete, the slobby wheelbarrows
lolloped over ramps, the screed work and shaky
gantries, the iron-welted paws and eye-scalding dust devils.

Fear bréige – 'scarecrow', 'straw man', 'man
who is false' – finally accommodated behind the basement
window of an inner-city dive, became
the incurious curiosity, a pine board for spine, a transverse
slat his arms at full stretch, a green-tinsel hair-mop

pinned under the hat, twigs of blackthorn his fingery jut.
Did he feel before the lads could the rumble
rising from the street, hear the new optimism, himself
a sounding board for economic boom?
No, he was entirely witless. Yet the boom came, rubbing

its hands, talking big, gathering force. Their
employer had a simple policy: just build an' be damned.
Payin' over the odds for materials anyways,
shake a leg, boys, shake a bloody leg. Windburn, sunburn,
frost and rain, they worked the hours he gave,

soon were coining. Could afford a posher place,
but the ingrained things held, touflish and hovel comforts.
Revelled on bleary Saturday nights – as galoots,
muck savages, hullabalooers; returned, spinning fictions
to fit the rags-and-wood man for a laugh.

It's how he earns his keep, they'd say, it's how he
minds the house. He wouldn't answer to that, or, if he did,
no one heard. Given a good kick sporadically
but couldn't take umbrage, and when the wrought-iron bath
grew cluttered with bean tins, beer cans, spud peel,

left-over T-bones, truce between them was a pretending
of blame on him. Slowly he gathered dust.
And they would dance rattling scaffolds of high-falutin hotels,
size up swing-a-cat mews, sort snag-riddled
apartments, guzzle their lunches in big galvanise boxes

whose walls were bare except for the cellotaped
and crinkling poses of Page 3 models, and whose exteriors
provoked a sideshow of scrawls of graffiti
daubed by local kids wiping their runny noses. Clear-outs,
dislocations, clutter of traffic countermanding

the hard-won communal thing forever at cross-purposes
with its own good intentions, its blundering fall down
humanity all messy and glorious in hard-knock
existence – none of that was their concern. Just doing me job,
they'd mumble to complainers, before moving

again, quick and rudimentary with shovel and barrow,
power tool, trowel, sandstone lorry. Some
could go through brick walls for a short-cut, others played
live-wire tamers in deadly earnest, more knew
how to make a hammer talk, a saw sing a song, dull wood

turn marvellous. One grew deft as a surgeon
in the ways he could swing and swoop a mammoth crane
on meticulous traverse of the gapped skyline.
So the asphalt thoroughfares gleaming with cat's-eyes
and whited demarcations whooshed into gear,

the peg-legged bridges spanned high and low, the ring roads
led onto ring roads, the thronged arcades
hoisted domes and unweary cupolas. Great constellations
of steel and glass across which sky and cloud
would abstractedly slide came to pass – sunlight's mill

and splintering a fierce bedazzlement. So the tall trees
let linger at the perimeter of each new venture
made a show of old-world maturity, though if you scanned
for a moment they might semblance only
stuntedness in face of the high-rise they were set against.

Most things went up precast monolithic, the votes
of corrupt servants of the people commodified
and biddable – secret, cash-stuffed envelopes, deals done
that could slew a shopping centre away
from neighbourhoods it was intended to serve, green-field

outskirts hurriedly rezoned and sectioned grey and pink
and yellow on maps in atria of council
planning departments. It was rock and roll, entrepreneurs
the new stars whirling their helicopters
above the heads of the commoners, shimmer of 'virtual'

fortunes, golf-coursed coastal rights-of-way, African
oil wells, pitch and toss of the markets assuaged
by insider tradings, moneymen and government ministers
privately tickling each other, tumescence
of bankers' bonuses, tease and titillation of social columns

in Sunday newspapers. How many ways can you sin?
Just one: by getting caught. Beatific republic
of the poor made to pay and scarcely visible the multitude
of true movers and shakers tasting only
their own sweat, uncelebrated struggle, honest and tenacious

as the overlaid, unloved, still-breathing humus.
Gazing of a morning with no food for the kids and no Santa
coming, a mother might stand skeptical of fairy lights
studded against a girdered sky – *Merry Xmas,
Yuletide Greetings* above her in-hock-to-the-lenders rooftop.

Seductive mantras, spin doctorates, financial analysts
luring the gullible, our 'spire of light'
a prideful focus, tallest sculpture grandstanding on God's
grunged earth, frenetic gaiety of youth
milling and sad youth gone flopping to grief, casual antic

of hoola-hoops slung over the upraised arms
of Big Jim Larkin, down the corner pub a gun fired, a hole
burned in a drug-pusher's heart. But would you
not feel disposed to slum in your Provençal summerhouse,
or breast the wavelets of goddess Shannon,

explore her Allen, Ree and Derg in your pleasure cruiser
if you were a powerful union leader, a big
company executive, or a tribunal judge goodly gracious
in long-winded deference to swindlers,
your retinue and argument of wizards conjuring a fortune

from the legal light show? Politicians skied
to a Rio conference on tropical rainforests, 'no women'
aboard the government jet, 'only wives',
and plaintive the head of the nation doesn't know
why all the cribbers and moaners won't go commit suicide.

Plush hotels two a penny now turning empty, houses
foundering – o rainy isle – in rivered hollows,
their pipes burst, veneers cracked, jambs and architraves
gone to rot, slipshod manufacture, exposure
of multitudes whistling for their supper the unavailing

warranties, while the quick and easy cover-all
cover-nothing of cliché plausibly hums the burst balloon
of the golden egg of the arse of the goose
fallen out of the bucket. No waylaying old ghosts, penury
and emptiness, shivering home to haunt the dream.

As for our red-neck heroes with dirt caked
under their nails, those laid off big boots – well, pundits say
it's the nature of casual labour to take what's
available, to stomp expendable and unnecessary away
when job's done, to keep an ear out for the boom

that might give them a start elsewhere. Diaspora again, our
favourite chatter word. While the very rich,
whose country is all countries and whose nation is none,
save themselves a cosy refuge, scurry after
their squirreled profits, trailing hard-done-bys and promises

to bounce back stronger than ever. But the fear bréige,
grown weary perhaps of doom and droning
pessimism, thumped and clumped his two wooden feet
up step by basement step, out the streets,
across the fields, over freshet rivers back to the ground

where he first saw the light of barley flowing. There the crows
flap about him undaunted as before, land
on his head and caw in raucous glory, heedless of his story
and unimpressed equally by the unvarying
shape, the one and only, he ever seems capable of throwing.

Groundswell

The Apples

They soon rot. But the shed where they've been heaped
stays upright for a hundred, two hundred years.
Our forebears plod in and out or, lulled to heavy-headedness
in that twilight, forget themselves and their errands
before coming to, fields away, one arm long as the other –
Van Winkles in hobnail boots and shabby coats
levelling at the gable their half-abashed curses. Until, through
trick or treat of seasons, the shed achieves disuse
and the curiously commonplace status of invisibility.
Nettles and ivy prosper; purple-stemmed briars
sway sharp-thorned across the slates. A hungry stranger
narrows one eye, sees things beyond things. His
bulldozer clunks and clangs – the stonework suddenly gives.
The unregarded seeds, thrown to frost and rain,
astonish him and us by sending up shoots. Wild apples,
on that account liable to stray from the character
of the parent. Still – progeny of an extinct breed – the cuttings
are sheeted in misty plastic and kid-gloved away
to a more favourable environment. We get no word back
of their propagation, but here the rough ground
swells, branching and blossoming and fructifying until a grove
of Hesperus develops. Patched ruddy and green,
the apples' meagre size is compensated for by their abundance
and the zesty, unsullied flavour that tangs and tingles
our taste buds. We hesitate only about swallowing the pips.

Soft Rushes

In each soft rush plant, the potential to grow
an entire soft rush city, and in each
soft rush marsh, buried under a gristly carpet
of rhizomes that creep and propagate,
a multitude of soft rush seeds

dormant in their beds. What we get
is the coverall effect of green and rusty colours
from a distance, the swish as we push
through them, the tussocky ankle-twisters
beaten here and there, and then an urge has us

reach in, as though we are children
venturing again, adroitly hunkering our bodies
to occupy the 'forms' vacated by hares.
Yes, soft rushes, never much to look at, still
made impressions that would last –

we heard before we could see the pheasant
shoot up out of its rangy camouflage,
immediately lost track of the snipe's gear-shifting
direction-changing scatter for the blue;
we took Callows water's refusal to take a hike

as our reason for dawdling around
shaky ground, or leaped where streamlets broke,
or followed after the marsh fritillary's go-
where-you-will. Or singled a rush to chew on,
unsheathed it to the white root, let it

dangle off our lips as we said slow things
in droll disparagement of our school,
or said nothing, being much too deep for words,
or wondered how in blazes men
such as us could be expected to plait a cross –

'add a soft rush to the right, then angle it
to the left' – for the Feast of St. Brigid.
But for all our loitering, we grew older, grew away
from the domain of *Junctus effusus,*
while behind us our fathers and mothers –

'modernising' as best they could – tried
to trample it, mow it, burn it, plough it, drain it,
even poison it, though in their hearts
they knew what their sorry heads had been taught
to disremember: soft rush always recovers.

Dead of Night Love Poem

There are sounds you make, sleeping, that keep me awake.
In the darkness I wonder if your dream will sunder you –
it seems to want to – gentle heave and great heave-ho
nestle there, or wrestle. We found we knew each other well
even at the beginning – so wed upon a Claddagh ring,
our bodies quickened to the deed's fulfilment of pure need.
You flummox me now in this: that our goodnight kiss
gives to a laugh or a sigh, a pleasure moan or a hurt cry.
I lie rigid in my unrest for fear a move might make distress
of what may be your delight, yet here beside you uptight
I wonder if some nightmare holds you trembling in its snare.
On and on we drift till daybreak – you asleep, me awake –
but when with morning you stretch, when you reach
and rummage across the mattress for your scattered clothes
and casually wriggle into them, then I begin to dream
you a picture of health, pellucid both in meaning and in pelt,
and in that amazed space nothing can hold me helpless
or send you harm though you go out to all the waking alarm.

Divination

He has eyes only for the ground as he paces slowly
to and fro. The forked rod of hazel,
gripped two-handed out before him, aquaplanes idly
on air. We hear the grass swish to his boots
tales of its perennial hold over everything.
And just when thirst for fresh sound or event
is about to disengage us, the rod twitches,
twists. More and more he wrestles until directly above
the pull of currents that has him in its grip.
He gasps; the skin on his face is drawn appallingly
downwards. We see him age twenty years
in that moment transfixed. The solid sight of a JCB
opening earth confirms his arcane bequest.
The wellhead is primed where the rod planted itself.

Scripture of the Wood

Outside, screens flickering, sirens and lights, whoosh of cars
I hear echoed in waterfall and in wind-fetched foliage
above my head. Here, no fashions, no celebrity –
ivy the only welcome mat. Talent shows feature nest birds
singing for their supper, reality TV for them a case
of live or die. But such hours I spend, stooping to decipher
the scripture of the wood, taking to a stalk
that's leafless, with six red berries up to no good, or angling
to get my head around a broken-off branch –
the leaves brown and wrinkly as bats before a sudden squall
riffles and flurries them into coppery coins spinning
in concerto. Lichens, a language for the fingers, an aesthete's
dapple, attest by their rich rusts and yellows
that the air is clean, while stinkhorn, lord of the flies,
simultaneously rebukes my nose. Cat's-cradle midges, the snail
drawing its seal across damp moss, scattergun ants
opening towards one purpose: these are my news.
And as I drowse, the trees – tall-cold, greenly cooking the sun,
patenting leaf and branch – transform to musket-stocks
in a dream, to furnace mills, to ships sailing
the lost centuries. But if civilisation's aggrandising harness
sweeps on to the breaking limit, a wood still standing
at the heel of everything proposes a book such as old Prospero
might fill with magic: which is to say life happening,
turn by turn of its deep-dimensioned pages, hill and stream
vivified – fish, feather, fur and leaf surviving as
they did before ever I appeared, as they will do though I leave.

Cloistered Man

The bronze head had its ear to the ground
in the Closter zu Allerheiligen, starry weeds were creeping
over it, and wasps rummaged fiercely

amid the fragrant petals, but the holes and tubular folds
of the iron eyes and mouth and lips
appeared to me a padlock for the earth, and the flat pipe

of the nose I imagined a key to a labyrinth
where everything destined to emerge – crocus, worm,
badger, oracle – would be free to do so

in its own good time, imbued with the gist and the mystery.
But even as my mind wandered off with this notion,
Rudolf Blätter's creation held firm, as if

listening out or listening in, and then the word 'spring'
brought me back again, though plainly spring
had come and gone, now down about the garden

the white blossoms of the giant 'schmurbaum' were falling,
bits and pieces beginning to cover the cloistered
man and – if I could but see – beginning to cover me.

Golem

Watch him building slowly for years, mounded up
out of mowed grass, lopped branches, ivy
strips, even thick bones which the dog couldn't crunch.
Scrutinise his under-parts already turned to clay.
Wolf-spiders caressing his forehead in warm weather,
gauze of bluebottles, earthworms ingesting
the place where rain seeps and lodges – his fecund belly.
Idly as an indulgent parent allow your hand
stained with spilt chlorophyll, snot-glue of crushed
celandine, lift to ease back his unruly dandelion fringe,
his hay-mopped head from the wall he leans
against, and then and there the smooth pebbling
of snails studded in their hundreds tells you
how blessed, what bliss to them his nurturing shelter.
Or woodlice spilling where his mossy sleeve's
unravelled by the wind, or a ruby and blue butterfly
alighting on the freshly cut nettle of his eyebrow.
Someday he will have grown powerful enough, you say,
to restore the barren back end of the garden,
the soil-stripped lip of a long worked-out quarry.
Meanwhile, fortnightly in season, you feed him the works
and rakings of good ground, year after year feel
your steps slow, the weight of mortality bring you closer
to the last breath you would bestow on him here,
that he might move, might decently bury you forever.

Sweeping the Chimney

You work rods and brush, knacks, angles, tactics.
A tarpaulin sheet with a hole in it splits.
Granite fire-bricks peek. A wrought-iron grate
at your heel upends. Downpour of soot
commences. Twig-clatter, tumble of jackdaw eggs
won't deter, nor yet the sweat breaking
on your brow. For you delve in a reverie
of discovering the first fire; you dream the nights
that charm, a cosy hearth to which, safe
and sound, you and yours always return. But still
the whispering soot insists there's a limit
to the number of nights. Your children
grow away. Their shoes and books and CDs,
casually scattered as if no greater displacement's
ever to happen, soon must be tidied for good.
And fret takes root, making you push through
to the top sunlight, the give that happens when you
least expect. So you collapse forward,
whistling softly to the thin chimney listening out.

The Burning Bush

"Look," you say, "the burning bush." And there
it stands on a rise before us, aside from the sweep of the river –
this tree transformed to autumnal splendour.

Shaking in its slender, supple twists, not one leaf
fallen yet, tinctures of pink and gold dappling and dancing air
and light, greens and whites relenting

to combustions of russet and searing crimson. Maybe this
is as close as we get, in a damp climate
turned deluge – with a torrent tearing across

the kitchen floor and a boat ferrying people down the street –
to comprehending Moses all agape before the bundle
of flames that were celestial or made celestial

by some old Biblical master of hyperbole. But you
and I move close enough to majestic to be getting along with,
clear-eyed still about each other, our heat

engendered in romanced body and thought,
and still with an eye for nature – fiery leaves on a trembling tree
finding us tranquil in the throes of a drowning God.

Cinéma Vérité

The Rathmines Stella, completely shot of its twinkle, is inherited,
now that we've done with it, by the meek – our 'feathered
    street rats' –
who rise flurrying from their pink-toed prance, to the grid
of rectangular spaces high in the granite brickwork, their very
    own loft.
We imagine them as the brains of the edifice, hatching movie
    plots –
cinéma vérité, not fluffy romance – in that stony cerebrum.
And the doubtful delights of mould and fleapit itch come
    scurrying back
from years ago, the moral guardianship of the usherette
shining her torch among our kisses and gropes. Pigeon love,
dare we say this doesn't exist? – for look, they increase and
    multiply,
coo and preen, while their shelter, our forsaken den of dreams,
stays in the dark, no sunshine or exotic locations imaginable on-
    screen,
only dirt-stains and flimsy hammocks of spider-web hanging
where we watched the outlaw dismount from his het-up horse,
    the nurse
who'd seen too much of suffering administer a lethal dose,
the two soldiers play Russian roulette; – well, this audience roosts
unconcerned. The rumour of the street, a filtered whoosh, a
    beeping
car-horn, a gabble of voices behind us, won't stop them
settling for the night. And the plot-lines of our lives –
    seemingly shapeless,
certainly untellable – move as we move, past steel-shuttered
    shop
and railing-rounded park, our prospects inauspicious, more

a case of earning the next crust than gazing at stardust, less
   intrigue
on the Orient Express than finding change for the last bus, yet
   somehow
to do with love even to the grand, impossibly heroic gesture
we promise ourselves we would rise to in face of impending
   catastrophe.

Washerwoman's Lane

You find the wall bedevilled by grime. There's a graffito
of a bear daubed on the wooden door calling a halt,
twenty paces in, to all that's left of Washerwoman's Lane.
Somehow the name, and not the space bulldozers

are clearing for a supermarket, displaces the here and now
of petrol station and film-rental store: you go back
fifty years and more, to the sound of worsteds pounded
in a bucket, scrubbed against a gridded board, the slop

of water onto path gravel. Your mother stoops, rinsing
fabrics, running them through a mangle. You see a small boy
cradling a book, with mites that move amid its must,
and broken bindings begun to spill its guts – he watches

on, beguiled yet condemned by her approval of his croon,
his making light of such syllables as would conceal
'skivvy', 'backache' and 'knuckle pain' behind the 'cloths
that billow blithely despite the inopportune falling of rain'.

Maquette

Heavy-headed and holding to a foetal curl,
your man of sculptor's clay, dried
in the sun where he's been left as though forgotten,
has taken also his share of rain
on board, and wept his burnt-sienna colour

down the windowsill, wept a great slow splash
of himself over the pebble dash –
until now, sundering and mouldering
in the little net-wire cradle that
contains him, he stirs in us feelings of pathos

we might prefer to do without. A flower
in its pot, standing near, melts back
after its fashion to a green slime, a primordial
soup, with suggestion of some fresh
new thing to come. And in the scummy water

of a sprinkler can, tiny creatures
wriggle through summer's fester, ascending finally
to the surface, fledged for take-off.
But still my eye goes back to this maquette,
finding him peculiarly compatible. His bulbous

skull, the vulnerable, buttony slope
of his neck, the rib-cage resembling a ruptured basket,
the rounded elbows, kneecaps arcing
loose, the knuckles and tarsals
begun to flute and crumble outward – is he

an effigy of the skeleton we found
in a disused quarry years ago, whispers of dust
sifting in and about, and what foul play
still buried? Or maybe he stands
for the boy who kicked a ball along the Liffey

one time it had frozen over, one time when fires
were lit on the ice – was it 1338,
or earlier, or later? Truth is, each visit
he represents the first thing that comes into my head.
I make-believe he has known small

sensate grandeurs, advance of moss
all down his chest and groin, lichen's cosmetic gloss,
the silken strings of a diadem spider's web
glistening where they rise about him
until it seems he is hoisting a shield or a trophy

up from his ankles and knees, past
his elbows, to the point of his chin. And known,
even as he sags and deteriorates, theatrics
of wild weather, brilliant bursts
of birdsong that haunt our living, moonshine

and starlight and the crimson glow
of the city sky provoking us to wonder late at night.
I allow he's shared your hand's touch,
in his rawness resisted this, much
as I still resist the shape you make of me.

And accept, as he disintegrates, images
of mourning he calls to thought – the refugee
from war, child of famine, victim
of contagion that is eventually all our human lot,
the dead one sent down the river in a boat.

Riviera

The white, close-crammed tables and deckchairs
on the private beaches at La Croisette
are anybody's now the patrons have gone indoors.

Onshore breezes caper the fine-gold sand,
sparing no footprint. The Carlton, the Marriot
and the Majestic shimmer behind us.

A bed for the night, breakfast excluded, would exhaust
our life-savings. The pier, beaded with lights,
resembles an ocean liner, or a yacht owned

by a Russian oligarch and moored where
it's deepest, at Antibes. Three flares of sanctuary-lamp
red, a moment's pause, three flares more:

we watch the Cannes lighthouse repertoire.
And exaggeratedly dance each other up Palais steps
the stars take to wave to flickering multitudes,

and exaggeratedly dance each other down
to follow far-flung peasant tales: of Estella the witch,
whose potions distilled from Alpine flowers

helped childless women to conceive; of Patrick
on the island of St. Marguerite climbing a palm tree
to evade the floods sent by God to flush out

a plague of snakes; of sheep descending the mountain
at dusk in pre-tourist Aix to drink from
the lovers' fountain. "Il pleut," you say, but still we go,

by train and bus and splashing through pavements
to see Matisse's Chapelle du Rosaire
de Vence. It's closed, wouldn't you know, so we ponder

la vie, la grande illusion, on our stroll back towards
sea level, while smoke from a rich man's
rubbish dump mingles with rainclouds high on the hill.

Drowning Machine

Things going down and coming up
and going down again. A leather football,
a leg of furniture, an umbrella's
spiky silver spokes with the black pleating
of its canopy still trying to open.

You say you could spend a day,
a season, a lifetime gazing into the churn
of the drowning machine. The weir
at eye level suggests you step back, choose
a wider angle. There, all's tranquil,

glassy in its casual, compelling over-brim.
And there, water's thrash, harsh
yet whisperful, effortless yet burdened –
a white 'shatter' through which
your mind turns its own fluid animal

and commotion of mysteries. Somehow
the promise of abated fuss is enough,
jingle of keys no longer missed, the day job
and its responsibilities exchanged
for slow walks, aloneness, unscheduled

stops and starts. To stay looking
is to dream a poem where old ghosts rise:
once-wild, once-roamed wetlands
given to marsh chalets and floodplain houses
whose cracked paraphernalia

in mud-moider suffer desolately empty.
And, fresh-faced, the parents
who sent you out, who beckoned you back,
so self-possessed you thought
the silent, sweeping arc of eternity itself –

star-twinkling on stiller waters –
would never carry them completely away.
Things going down and coming up,
fishermen careless that they catch nothing,
bats spinning, a blood-red streetlight

taking charge of its element. You dither
between distances at either hand,
quit the main road for the leafy way. It looks
equatorial but is simply nightfall,
local trees darkening in their valley stand.

Lydia Jumped

And if a startled bird flew up, or if a branch creaked
in the wood, was this the same as if nothing
had happened? We'll find pleasure again on the banks
of the brown Dodder; we'll walk next the spate
and open our minds to the thundering waterfall. Again
when the river clears, we'll see our faces laughing
in its untarnished mirror. We'll wear lilies
about our heads in that reflection. But not today.
Because Lydia jumped today, to stop the hurt – maybe
a silence or a fist, maybe a word – to stop
the hurt she never uttered, who now might shrug
at our notions of respect for the dead, and wonder why
we can't more cherish the living instead.
O do you say she hovers still between the tree canopies
and the watercourse, taking time out to pity us?
Do you sense how she contests her own fading sense
of the streetlamp and the moon, two splintering
silver sickles afloat? Can you pluck from
thin air the tiny goodbye she waves to the fixture that is
a heron fishing? Or to the pair of swans,
'the stupidest swans in Dublin', nesting on a temporarily
dry segment of the sweeping weir? Glean
what you may, Lydia's gone, and no heaven or earth,
no cypress wreath affixed to the iron footbridge
with her name on a card dampening above the spindrift …

Belmont Mill

A kingfisher on the Brosna finds himself taken – with the river –
indoors through an arch and along the headrace
of Belmont Mill. Whispers and sibilances flowing below
are barely audible compared to the gushing weir he was said by
a wing-beat ago, and if all else about the mill
sits quiet and still, no thump from the breast-shot waterwheel,
no drip or spill into the flume, this 'halcyon'
in his confusion just doesn't know to go back the way he came.
But we make ourselves at home, poke our noses
in the kiln and our fingers in the holed and heavy tiles that once
hotly dried the grain, plant our feet on the broad
boards of the granary and find delight in the sluice gate's rattle,
the start of an old commotion. A water-turned world,
the marvellous articulated in the basic: spindle
and spur, pit wheel and wallower, the burly transfer of power,
swish music of the shelling stone, turf flavours
tasteable in the pinhead oatmeal. And, emerging out of folklore,
out of the deep-seated remembrances stored
in things, the stone-dresser treats the grindstone, furrows it, so,
with his double-sided bill, tiny fragments flying off
into the flesh of his arm a proof he's up to the job, able to show
his metal. With now the play of light against dust,
the shadows and echoes close to ethereal, and the mill's first
guest, the kingfisher, gone ahead of us as he has done
before, as he will do again, through a window specially left open.

Taken with Gooseberries

Over at Shiel's old stone house, with its low roof
and the long chimney lifted from a fairytale,
a clutch of scratchety bushes. Their fruits feel solid,
resiliently pneumatic. The hispid skin
is yet translucent enough to see through to the seeds.
They burst jelly-sweet between the teeth,
roll a rusty taste around the tongue. Ever after

I dote on gooseberries, let them be red or yellow,
green or white. But there in childhood
amid lodged grass a smothered bee-buzz, the world
whispering behind my ears its 'constant now'
of matter and scatter and breeze. I dream
nature's 'good deed' – the growing of gooseberries –
as my own endeavour. I want them heavier

than any other body's, a nurturing to be ensnared by
as I lean over net wire deep in some
slow shire. I go to sleep with berry secrets. Weep
to find the biggest berry weeping; blame
frost; blame hand-heat – my unmet wife's or my own.
Turn nervy, act stand-offish as I watch
the scrupulous witness seal the few I've plumped for

in a box. And dream of prize-giving day,
a tiptoe towards where the scales balance the berries
singly up – clop of pennyweight counters –
while about me autumn conducts its slow lapse,
each side-tracked thing tangling the next, thistledown
filling an old sandpit, growth and die back
and such rag trees in mind I'm never done shaking.

The Night as in Her Hair

To be possessed of a floral clock even if you are no flower
is advantageous. To know enough
to close down when the fun's waning and the party's over
can save you from tiff or kafuffle, and many
a domestic squall. And just such a shortfall's borne

home to me in wind and rain tonight,
thinking about Carl Linnaeus of all people, how he threw
himself on his knees on Putney Heath
and exhaled a 'thanks be to God' first time he clapped eyes
on glorious, flowering furze. Carl, who made fresh

and clear the sexual arrangements of flowers
in terms of brides and bridegrooms celebrating their nuptials
behind *soft scents* and *noble bed curtains*. Except,
I'm sure he saw, red-bloods come clothed
in complexities a flower can't rustle up, shifts or slips

beyond the seasonal, and harmony tends towards arguable
if not downright argument. But she and I
are apart where we should be together dreaming,
this hand mussing of its own accord the night as in her hair,
the sunrise of her breasts – double power – due

about two hours from now, the dawn chorus
founding itself on tiny clicks her throat makes when we
ride the transports of touch and pleasure.
Beggar's choice – hide among the wild, under the scathing
shelter of that bird-shaped, bandy-legged

fellow-outcast furze forever threatening take-off,
quell by salve and smell of its perfume my high dudgeon until,
more stealthily even than great botanists can tell, I crawl
and creep damply, greenly home where she
relenting twists and whispers me through the long dark lifting.

Foundlings

1
One or other of these half-feral cats
places a dead thrush or robin on the doorstep
some mornings as a way to my heart.

2
A spider coated a creamy colour
hides among the pale clotted petals of the rose –
you sniff the flower, sniff the spider.

3
Now he can scratch, the one gone
ages below asphalt and tailback and small talk,
the lost and found Devil's Toenail.

Daisy Cutters

Stalks lopped at a stroke of the crooked scythe
I didn't mourn – nettle, thistle, burdock –
but rather swung in an exultant arc
against the grain of everything that stood
in my path. And when the ground was won back,
I accounted it a personal cleansing.
Blithely imagining some brave act of soldiering
on a farm in the west, in a battle
with my brothers which, even today, we
don't declare. And I see him in the west that is
more vast by far, this boy from Idaho
swinging his scythe, relishing the long-drawn
munch of cut foliage, the whetstone
and the sun. This young man destined not to make
a living from the land. This soldier
who drawls to me matter-of-factly now about
the capability of a weapon he saw
and still sees as his duty to put in motion – the war
zone, the spinning canister stationed
just above the ground, bomblets hissing as they
radiate out from it, lives and limbs
taken, the entire area swept, he assures me, clean.

The Birdman of Nicaragua

He whistles out the exact centre of his mouth birdcalls which
 birds
whistle back; and he will grin at the notion of himself
as the Birdman of Nicaragua, and sleep where the space
is rent-free, in a narrow shack islanded between two railway
 tracks —
all unperturbed though the wheels of a train took
one of his arms and one of his legs while he lay sleeping one
 night;
the same train that whizzes past him now, the same
or another, singing along a line to his left or along a line to his
 right.

Amputations

In the hospital he tells me how he thinks today to itch
the space where his foot used to be,
tomorrow to clip the toenail of that same foot.

I go to catch the smell of an apple
that doesn't exist, in a branch I prune, mid-November,
from an apple tree – I mean the sharp

rind-sap the nicked bark sprays into open
air and space, where will extend the branch differently,
the spur yielding blossom and blossom

giving apple, green apple, come summer.
In the act of pruning I consider how my friend, suffering
a malignant tumour, has had the leg

severed below the knee – and gradually the branches,
blighted by winter, cut back, cut away,
shape the tree as a cup set to fill with sunshine.

I meet him returned home and beginning
to recuperate in his garden. I wonder at his effort of joy
in watching fresh buds break palely. I'm

given to observing his silences around nightfall.
But the poem, when he utters it, rumbles
and rages: a bloody-minded, anger-struck, tumbling lyric.

It grunts and groans, its hard-pressed words prop
themselves up, honest as the stretch
in the evenings. And the tree – sporting apples now –

dances on in its seemingly stationary orbit,
heedless of everything save chemical ways of looking
at how to avail of space, how to harness light

without jumbling its branches. But where
I find replenishment in its freshly vigorous canopy, he
whose limb is lost – dealing as he must

in different gifts of sustenance – reaches, still reaches,
as if it will prove possible to answer
in a touch the ghostly tingle, the absent part of himself.

Red Deer Skull

Though it suggests the long face of a saint in a medieval painting,
it's still made to appear small, even incongruous,
by the many-tined antlers it bears. Antlers more rigid than alder,
yet full of the idea of spar and tangle as they refuse
any easy accommodation with my hands. And the red deer
    himself,
a king burdened by his crowning glory – there's that, at least,
to say to the boy who brought for classroom display
this weather-bleached specimen from where he found it, in a
    wood
near Muckross. There's the path evolution took,
turning tusks into branchy racks that – clothed with velvety skin –
grow in spring, and from *venari*, 'to hunt', there's venison.
But now I stand at the exit, my own semblance of solid or set
a front for all that flows. And these schoolchildren whose
    departure
I'm overseeing linger still to wrestle the skull's
primordial head-rig, to pull faces aping the empty eye sockets,
the thin 'handles' of the jawbones. Or simply to lean in listening
as though they can hear a last exhalation of breath,
a faint echo of the rutting season's roar. Fellow-feeling for a
    dead thing –
even a dead thing once considered a king – is not
a wonder to dwell on, but soon the houses in their pastel colours
materialise again, the afternoon traffic ratchets up a gear,
and somewhere in my care I rejoice at how lessons are unlearned
or broken, at how the noise and nurture run together
and sunshine in its deepening seems to promise life will go on
    forever.

Scut

Intoning 'a gift for teacher'? More a gruff "Here Mister,"
a winter of smokes and glue-sniffs
taking his voice, more a cracked tenderness as he
palms me this lightest of light surprises,
this fluffy white scut culled from the rabbit he shot
in open ground beyond Cherry Orchard.

"How could you?" is not a thing to ask,
despite the jump I get, for – enraged – he'll say I'm soft
in the skull, crying over a stupid rabbit,
and besides, the only qualms I can spare are to do
with the notion of a ten-year-old
shooting guns as part of his weekend entertainment.

Build a nature lesson around the rabbit's place
in folklore? It's no sustenance for a boy whose own place
is nowhere. And detailing the luck
associated with the rabbit's colour or with whether
this 'inspirer of myths' passes behind us
or before is to ensure he'll screw up his freckled nose

and the wrinkles creasing his brow just deepen further.
The rabbit as a symbol of fertility? –
momentarily he'll be all ears, then make quick,
copulatory gestures with his fingers, grin his knowing grin.
No, it is enough to accept the gift
and be thankful. For even if full of livewire impulses,

beating a path from one trouble to the next, he seems
scarcely to exist other than as an intense,
nervy hallucination – long-faced, feral child talking
in twitches and bursts, all short shrift, all mother's grief,

all set to run, his panoramic eyes scanning
the odds offered on cover blown, on flimsy camouflage.

Plastic Coal Sack

It becomes in turn a comet's arcing flight, a ghost
entangled among branches, a neon-lit bat,
even a tattered underpants. But still the high wind
that lifted it up and out of the garden
keeps blowing. Imagination will make so much
of a thing and then fall short, the moon
afford poor translucence to our thoughts as we watch,
frazzled by a constant flap – who would choose
instead a flock of finches dappling the tree,
a crop of apples festooning the space between us
and sunset, some sign of symbiosis or song
of greening, but who will settle yet for the wind's
abatement, the tilt and teeter and turning
iridescence of a magpie preening a long tail feather.

Crow Conversations

The grey-skinned quartzite cone of the Sugar Loaf,
crows flying over, lifting towards us, flapping
in their twos and threes at first, thickening then to scores,
multitudes deepening the darkness that brings
them about. There's money in rookeries, an old voice
offers, money and luck. I grew within earshot
of crow-haunts, my dawn and my dusk crow-capped.
I saw the starveling despatched by its parents,
and a parliament convened around the diseased, to kill it.
No use in nature for weak or withered
unless to feed off, stubby maggots making the carcass
move. Still we fall over and over in love
with 'mother' nature, the 'good' earth, 'innocence'
of birds and beasts, wax lyrical in spite of all we know
of the ravening behind everything – it preys on us, too,
it scavenges – but now again the flight of crows
over the Sugar Loaf to take their rest recalls
for me far rookeries girded up out of great horse chestnut
and beech trees that stand for home, first home,
crow conversations become the earth speaking in riddles
that stay unfathomed no matter how intently I listen.

The Tunnel

Bees and butterflies, once in, are unlikely ever to make out
the ramshackle door again. The polythene they throw
themselves at, towards the light that promises airy space, thwarts
to the point where – watching – we begin to attribute

to them feelings of frustration and despair, their repeated
actions quickening until, muzzy and spent, they settle
for the purple flower of a thistle opening here, the white cups
of bindweed on a mission to carpet the clayey floor.

Which still leaves this quandary of our own to sort – the live
weight of a few butterflies, a few bees tilting the scales
one more jot towards planetary survival or not, while all those
good intentions we started but haven't brought to fruit

lie with water hose and sprinkler can amid strawberry plants
in the drinkless dust, or find us leaning into that deep
dark emptiness when we lift the lid off the house for honeybees
and inhale the stale-chocolate odour of our childhood sins.

Brother

Two guinea pigs, unnoticed, ate your shoelaces even as you stood
making at the bench, and swallows flying about shaved your head.

Groundswell

Apollo did the dirt, slew poor old serpent god Python,
whose corpse gradually decomposed – the smell,
initially horrible, had tempered itself by the time
the Sibyl breathed it in, and was now an entrancing perfume.

Rubbish, say the experts, that Delphic whiff
was naturally occurring ethylene. But what a gas, still,
what prophecies came to shape the destinies
of peasants and kings trying to live up or down to them.

And if my wetlands will-o'-the-wisp must turn
to methane, or luminosities glissading my skin as I rise
from the turlough are to pass for algal
fluorescence, they've long since exerted their influence.

Here is ground and groundswell, fit matter
for a day's dalliance or a lifetime spent deliberately looking.
Here we speak to each other because of the river –
not the fact of the river but the mood it pushes,

the clay-coloured flood so deep the heron must step
aside from it, the water-hen retreat under St. Patrick's cabbage.
And, fresh as Hopkins saw it, 'Kingfishers catch
fire', their orange bellies flaring from a blue-plumed bush.

Imagining My Mother as a Sibyl

If she sits on a tripod communing with the earth's navel,
as did the wise women of Delphi
each in turn long ages ago, this is coincidental
to the task at hand, peeling spuds, for example, or milking.
A life's no less intense for being spent

in one spot; so charmed and charged she must look
about her, always curious. And wander
the wetlands in her rainbow scarf and moss-green coat,
and ramble again in her mind alone
until she is ready to go ghosting on her final journey.

A spring well glimmers in her eye; she
will follow cracks in the kitchen floor back to where
her children are infants; or – dipping into a rabbit's burrow –
find a rogue egg laid by a rogue hen,
an intact yolk in a thin-skinned sac, completely

devoid of a shell. Her chestnut curls
turn slowly grey and the roses in her cheeks wither gently.
Her mind stays quick. She'll lose only if she must
her pragmatic farmer self and give its due
to the 'flaggard' flowering yellow and purple, which she

never once dreams of calling iris. And from
'sibyl' no less than 'navel of the earth' make her amused,
vaguely puzzled retreat – not raving or falling
into a trance, not offering any huge pronouncements
to shake the world or change its course,

no allegory or embellishment, only the names and faces
recurring, vivified in fond, fierce whispers
as she departs with the blameless over meandering
streamlets and old stone bridges, towards
where will-o'-the-wisp holds out for her promised dance.

Yeti

Sunlight dazzled the rushy rink of the turlough. A blackthorn
snapped. I lifted a discus of ice from a barrel
and flung it at the row of cypresses shouldering their
blue-green shawls. The whiff of foliage scorched by coldness –
I seldom catch it now, and always only as grief
for my own slipping resilience. Or maybe for the imagination
of the child who saw a yeti, that day, climbing
the chimney of a far, whited rooftop – a child whose sudden
transmogrification of snow so freaked his bones
he thought to outrun the lumbering mammoth of the Callows.

Wetland Elegy

Each unfettered, undiluted fairytale came true for me in a well
where wishing, and not the wish fulfilled, worked every spell.

I chased a fox down a burrow, only to glimpse him again
up on his hind legs at midge-struck evening, strolling as a man –

there, in a leap, he reverted to animal. A river meadow
sang me its prince, even if I croaked the frog's basso profundo.

On the wheeze of wild-geese wings, flurry of wild-geese cries,
I was transported, with Kay and Gerda, to meet the Queen of Ice.

But today, oil bursting uncontrollably from under the sea,
brings back – amid these pastures drained for rye – the memory

of skirting a quag's thick gruel, and all that seemingly ran
to living plenitude, as though Callows was a bottomless saucepan.

An Afterlife for Animals

Those wildings hunted to extinction, their whuffles,
chirrups and whoahs reverberating in our ears
the primordial earth full of suffering and full of ancient
healing laughter; those birds of paradise flown,
the flaring electric hues of their plumes
appearing less resplendent than ridiculous in the hands
of milliner and trophy hunter now; those
in pelts ranging from dawn-soft to sunset-streaked
to quenched midnight – maybe one day
they'll be retrieved as holograms for our grandchildren,
put through their paces in some simulated
habitat, tended and befriended by way of compensation.

Wind Chimes

Chime on, you tell me, and I will, though my tinkling
is out of fashion, though the wind, random
tuner of everything, has given our garden to silence
and a threat of rain. But you, who've gone
making art as you must do, put your voice to my ear
and lip-paint *Goose Egg and Belleek China*
into my imagination, while damselflies and kingfishers
colour your words where you stroll beside
a faraway canal. Keep chiming, you say, and I, trying
gallant that I am, lightly touch my fingers
off these tubular garden bells strung outside the window.
The 'five silver chimes of Mercury' the logo
on the wind-catcher describes them, but no quibble,
Mercury's a god after all, fleet messenger
of the gods and goddesses, and if he carries a wingèd stick
and not a musical device, let the liberty
happen still in lieu of wild and winsome words
I compose for you but am slow to whisper now or here –
about the lives filled to overflow I dream us
together going through – let the chimes draw you near.

Divje Babe

Do, re, mi, fa. Taphonomists and musical archaeologists
play the conundrum of the Divje Babe bone flute –
a bear-cub femur into which a wolf long ago sank its teeth;
or in which a Neanderthal tribe scooped holes
so they could tootle tunes in the cave that gives it its name?

Now though we rave or boogie all night in low-down dives,
or levitate respectably to opulent orchestrations
of sound gods at La Scala or Boston Symphony Hall, or find
ourselves sent, as we sit at home, by mellifluities
of harpoon and axe and modern equivalent of a perforated

Pleistocene mandible, the experts – promulgators
of labels and lists, reciters of the 'proper' constituents of jazz
or rock or country blues, meriters and demeriters
of commercial versus artistic success – are never far. I push
the head-bothers aside, hang loose-limbed-tender

until someone poses the question: "I wonder if all the music
started there?" So I let myself be drawn into this
suggestive, cool-sounding cave, Divje Babe, into deliberation
on the bone flute as the oldest musical instrument
ever uncovered, into arguing the flute's length against its ability

to caress two or more octaves, the roundness of its tone holes
for fingers and how appositely varied the spacings.
Oh brother, all I want to say is blow; oh sister, do what you do.
Let me be a caveman down with time since the first
tap, click, clap, mumble. The day I stop, pick over my bones.

The Dead Petitioners

We enter a grey cathedral whose tombs of soldier noblemen
lie since the 13th century coldly silent, and each outline

of a knight in armour depicted in relief, with his sword
at his side, fingers closing around it, still leaves the last word

to a stone dog curled next his feet, or to the etched faces
of six apostles signifying that the beneficiary of their grace

lived and died *in the service of God and Country*. Brief
existence – triumph and title, political acumen, personal grief –

is scrolled on marble plinths; but rather than sigh
in prayerful sorrow for the dead petitioners, rather than cry

at life's futility, citing the evidence set unwittingly down,
we go out to the blow of bracing air and rain, the busy town

that slows to allow us pass, grateful and unknown, along
alleyways and side-streets lifted in the five senses of our song.

Ireland's Eye

Mr. Ferguson rowed the shop-girls out to Ireland's Eye
for a daytrip in his boat, a decorous picnic
early in the summer of 1938. What did they talk about?
The threat of war in Europe? The tale of the woman
who was murdered on the island in 1852? No,
they surely agreed a splendid day for boats and picnics.
And visited the old church and the Martello tower.
And found the idea of ducks nesting in rabbit burrows
peculiar, even off-putting. And marvelled at the Stack,
that big, spiky mollusc of a rock. And heard
the gabbing din of many flocks – tern, guillemot, gannet,
razorbill – which Mr. Ferguson must have taken
pains to name. Probably the girls giggled about everything
later – including the knots and stresses soft-hesitant
in Mr. Ferguson's voice. But there and then, when all
was still in keeping with genteel convention,
they naturally made a show of pinching their noses against
the fishy smell of seabird colonies coming up the hill.

Fastnet

People give fresh names to your 'sharp-tooth'
of the Old Norse – 'Eye of Europe'
a welcome sight for sailors bearing homewards
off the Atlantic; 'Ireland's Teardrop'
the exiles' wistful glance back; 'Lonely Rock'

your isolation on all but rare pet days.
You outlast tide-swells, storm fleets shredding
rain sheets against your serrated pinnacle,
mist and fog fuddling your lighthouse. Third
super structure, this, the initial edifices

rickety things of brick and cast-iron
that even your clay-slate and quartz foundation
couldn't hold propped. Lamp-tenders
have suffered your cramped space, you in return
remained steadfast through their vigil.

But such tales the keepers could tell
of the sea and its shapings, of sights they found
inexplicable. Card games and chess
to lighten moods of slowly drawn loneliness,
the rising boom beyond rounded wall

turning frenzied, wraithful, a behemoth
throttling even your hard neck, jittering teacups
off their kitchen dresser and table.
Panicked thoughts leant against, sea-roar
and sea-roar's subsidence, quietness happening

to get the hang of itself, hearts lifting in abated
fret, hands assembling square-rigged
model ships as gifts for family and friends – tug
of heartstrings implicit in thin threads
hoisting to sail each flimsy vessel inside a bottle.

Calm heroism of James Kavanagh, stone mason,
forgetting his own safety or health as he set
an elaborate joggle of dovetails in place
for the new lighthouse – strict yet intimate lock
of binding blocks become the handling

of more than two thousand rocks, double this
the tonnage weight – a plumb-line dropped
from the tower-top to you as the base
showed barely one whit out of true vertical.
And though decades pass his purposeful colossus

endures, your name claimed now as its own,
and where you end or it begins is bubbled
with bladder-wrack. Behind you both we envision
the long watch faithfully kept – back
and back to the first filling of St. Dubhdán's

fiery iron basket, through dim antiquity back
to the Pharos of Alexandria, further
through far-flung makeshift lookouts our forebears
raised on snag-shelved shore. Forward
towards us, so, imagine the voyagers plotting

their course, wavelets illumined by wood
and coal and charcoal furnace, by oil
and electric and solar power – and though today
your lighthouse, programmed to bellow
and to cast its eye, suggests the keeper's exploits

are over forever, still a boundary and a bulwark
ranges against the tempestuousness
of the ocean, still shipwreck happens, still the ship
shakes free of storm-surge and abyss
to navigate each hazard on which the sea breaks.

The House of the Fire

On Inishmurray they kept a fire going in a hole in the floor
of 'Teach na Teine', or rather it kept itself,
through grace of St. Molaise, their forebear. Long before

matchsticks and Zip lighters and balled-up newspaper,
when smooring hot coals with ashes
last thing at night didn't guarantee live cinders in the morning,

the islanders could visit the fire store and blaze up
their turf sods there. For centuries this
kept them sure. Until a visitor – worldly-wise or rebellious,

or maybe just bored to impetuousness – decided to piss
on the saint's fire as a disproof. Well,
the flames leaped, a furnace consuming him, starting

at the groin. His last few blackened bones
were bundled into a nook in the wall of the house of the fire
and kept for display and cautionary purposes.

Whether or not the fire ever did exist, or the young man
demonstrated his disrespect, or died for it,
the dark-minded comedy seems to run true to our subverted

history. But Inishmurray, bereft of its people,
isn't bothered how we converse with ourselves or with each other
among the silences here, between the gaps

in breezes and the gaps apparent in everything everywhere.
We're free to fan or douse what fires we may
from the shards of modernity, the scatter of island memory.

Natural History

The last act of the huge pike – to swallow almost whole
a smaller rival. Which, before it dies, digs its way
half-through the gills of its attacker. Both specimens

float now in a formaldehyde jar, conflicted in one hunger
and one space for us to abhor, or find the nerve
to admire. Or there's a spaghetti ball of thread worms

extricated from the gizzard of another creature,
inducing a shudder. Or a wasp that makes a living larder
of the tarantula, so its own larva may survive.

On and on the dreadful devices, the live-or-die scenarios,
until we wonder if all's a case of cannibal existence
precluding redemption, and are shaken – as Darwin was –

out of the consoling notion of God as benign apotheosis
to which we aspire. Throw warfare into the hat,
throw barbarities we wage against earth and each other,

still somehow our morose hearts hold there exists a heaven
beyond the sway of instinct and natural wildness,
beyond the special sorrow saved for us, the aspirant angels.

Plague Bodies

When they tumbled the plague bodies, tangle of limbs
and lolling skulls, into a pit on Lazzaretto Nuovo Island,
in or around 1576, they must have known
they would need to make a return visit, dig the earth
open again to cope with a fresh epidemic.
A bite from a flea infected by a rat, or the way contagion
travels by means of the air, merest inhalation
of viral breath – they knew nothing of that, superstitious
and struggling along their journey. And they
had to return. The diggers earned their corn. The grave
reopened gave off its festering stench.
Decomposing corpses – one swollen, with blood
rimming its lips. "Vampire," they shouted. "She hides
among the dead. Look how fat she is; she's
bitten through the shroud we put about her face."
So they 'starved' her by forcing a stone between her jaws,
and thus she was uncovered in our time,
no vampire there, everything made explicable as science
will allow: bacteria, build up of fluids and gases
resulting in her ghoulish appearance – still we gape back
through dark to darkness of plague and pustule,
to the dying droves whose ignorance didn't make for bliss,
and find the potential for nightmare ever-present, enlightenment
breaking slowly no matter what distance or how
promisingly we advance, and sorrow for the credulous
forebears, the child in all of us, falling among our thoughts.

Soyer's Recipe

The soup boiler sits rust-eaten under a hedge, moss
cosying up to its lip and nettles scraping
an existence out of the black abscess at its base.
It doesn't hold water any more, but we imagine water
there – approximately two gallons, frothed
by morsels of leg of beef, a few diced onions, a pinch
of salt admixed to a shake of brown sugar,
with pellets of pearl barley floating on the surface.

Soyer's Recipe for outdoor relief: 1s 4d the cost;
'prudent economy' – the lumper, the rock,
the Irish Apple and the cup, all rotted where they lay.
But if today the leaf-dappled shadows reveal
no starving figures shivering, no bone bundles heaped,
no fevered heads wobbling on withered stalks,
the museum at Strokestown tells their story –
the stain of human famishment in which, however

unwittingly, we are complicit as it seeps onward
and down. For long after the voice-over has held us
rapt and sorrowful, the figures still stumble
across our thoughts, appear unbidden on our screens,
fed to us in small doses and rations, the fly-covered
orbs of their eyes beyond beseechment
or tears, their faint breaths squeezed by imperatives
of sky rockets and 'smart' weapons, trade

tariffs, food mountains, casual wastes and neglects
that bring them to expire. So we weep, well-meaning
as before, and weep the more at each tidbit
fleshing out their desperate chronicle. So the blamed

soup boiler is mobilised and stirred one way
or another. And a tent flaps somewhere and a field
logistics officer mutters *Fuck it; fuck it to high
heaven* as clay is shovelled over the coffinless corpses.

At Pompeii

They put the words 'Cave Canem' on a mosaic
outside the House of the Tragic Poet.
Today it draws a smile, as elsewhere the fresco
of a man with two penises, blithely
advertising the local 'lupanare' or brothel.

We walk the basalt streets, tourists taking in
each excavation, not thinking charnel
or incinerator, simply enjoying the sun, the sense
of theatre affirmed by brooding Vesuvius
standing wisps of steam against the blue horizon.

And nothing troubles or touches us
until this effigy of suffering made explicit,
this cast of a bronze-collared hound
flung upwards writhing, his jaws agape as when
he was caught by a blast of fiery air,

a plaster wrought of his last posture and elevated
at an angle where he twists, his forepaws
seeming to join, to make the shape of a prayer.
But then the 'Fugitives in the Garden'
fleeing 'early on the morning of the second day'

into a dead end where they tried to find shelter
impel us towards them, one man
propped on elbow, his last act
imaginable as defiance against the exploding firestorm,
while in another place the figure lying

with his hands clasped across his belly appears
to be asleep and blithely unaware,
or in yet another a semblance of Rodin's
The Thinker attends the man who sits
seeming to wipe a smudge of smoke or a teardrop

from his eye. Pliny the Younger's *'cloud
of unusual size and appearance ... like an umbrella pine,
for it rose to a great height ... and then
split off into branches'*, comes to mind – eerily
evocative of the nuclear mushroom that towers

a shadow over our own time. Still
we feel the urge to reach for the huddling multitude
held in the gloom that grows deep,
in the thunder of approaching cataclysm
that has them call, children to mothers and fathers

invoking the heedless gods for mercy. Still
we sail the doom boat in our imagination, with Pliny
the Elder from Misenum, whose wish
to make a scientific study is soon outstripped
by his desire to offer help. Against all advice

he steers his course. Inlet and promontory, altered
by the fall of pumice and molten ash, appal.
He stands wheezing on the shore until
overcome by fumes. We picture him lying peacefully
as if asleep. The mourner in us is found to weep.

Subterranean Song

Seumas O'Kelly's bedridden old Malachi Roohan twists
or wrestles somehow up, determined to settle,
once and for all, the proper site for the weaver's burial.

He grasps the rope tied to the bed's end rail, heaves
himself half-vertical in order to pronounce
on communal connectedness, on memory and source,

but more, on the dream nature of everything.
The task of location, which will prove beyond him,
is resolved finally in a comic quarrel involving two other

ancients, a nailer and a stone-breaker, only to stand
redundant next the budding love between
the weaver's youthful widow and a young grave-digger.

I sit, aged thirteen, turning the pages of my father's
far-out relative's magnum opus, and weeds
spring to mind, blood-barked yew trees and crooked

trellises of ivy. A pluck of dust happens where
herbs are tugged loose, and rhizomes that rip a sequence
of thin disturbances off the loamy graveyard ground.

A lone bush materialises, by which to lift
the grassy scalp of the ring-fort mound. I struggle down
to the subterranean, struggle and suffer

and snuggle into this dank and dismal yet strangely safe
reverse, this last recourse, bowels of the earth.
I smell humus and musk, sense something stirring – a wan

tendril or a rat's tail – while about my stultified head
clay molecules collude, mouldering the bones
of my placid bedfellows, the dead. Here, the stokers

of fires, the shapers of farms and folktales.
Here, the famine priest's vestments, which a mechanical
digger is destined – years from now – to raise

in pristine preservation, to set as hastily back,
after we rumple with our fingers a thing made marvellous
in the village mind. And here, unsullied

in its delft pot, the butter that was churned more than
a century ago, which the girl next door will
declare edible, touching it with a finger onto her tongue.

Seasons

Though physical desire between them must die
is what even lifelong lovers say, and though their desire –
as if chastened – falls away, I see us kiss
in a room called enfeeblement that is small and bare
and entered by an old, creaky door. There
we undress, ignoring the tarnished eye of the mirror.
There we embrace. Seasons advance – from
winter's crippling cold to where plums cluster, dark
and luscious. From summer's piquant green
to ripe, sun-struck apples. So do sapless sticks flex
and fire themselves afresh to nodding heads
of roses fragranced red and orange and yellow rustling.
The big adventure of the earth rolls out over
one more year. It still can't match our fling. We hold
to our own spring, even in the thin, musty air
behind that narrow door – two sublime slips of a thing.

Song for a Centenarian

The world will forget us, Josie, though we hold –
as you do – to one place for a hundred years;
the world is busy forgetting us even now as you lose
your bearings, fall down brittle-boned
in your little kitchen among the limestone hills,
and can neither lift nor drag yourself out

to daylight again. The crookedly hanging clock,
stained with turf-smoke, grease-spattered
from the frying pan, makes itself audible to you
as if for the first time. The concrete floor
coldly props your hip pain. The simple
sufficiency of bread, of milk in a jug, of a jar of jam,

stands unreachable. One hundred years
of stout health – call it forbearance or good fortune;
call it the knack of knowing how to pick
your step; or maybe it's the quiet rapture of always
feeling at home. Still there's no sizing
or summing life up; your purgatory of slow seconds

gathers into hours, into days; your panic settles
almost to repose at the sight of moonlight
illuminating the badly distempered chimney breast.
And this isn't the last, the end of anything,
but a continuing story where you survive, courtesy
of a square-shouldered bottle of whiskey

squatting on a low shelf, which you judiciously sip,
your head resting on the belly of the world,
your ear attuned for our footsteps. And hope – shyly

yet indefatigably you give it quavering voice —
is a bird breaking into song at dead of night,
prompting a tree to rise in the haggard of your mind.

Geezer

To find in slowly ripened time you are old,
a fumbling and stooped curmudgeon
never picking the path of least resistance
even in the crucial, maddening matter
of articulating the right word that is always
on the tip of your tongue. To feel
justified in taking what pleasure you can
from noisily blowing your nose
into a plaid handkerchief, or from fiddling
with coins at a post-office counter
while the whole queue sighs lengthily behind.
Let them make allowance for diminished
circumstance; you roll and unroll
with the days, still able to tie your shoelaces
and shave your face. And the supposed
liberations of being an old geezer? You'll say
they are mythical, to be endured
as a thousand tethers tightening their grip,
bearable provided you can get away
even for a day to watch the waves breaking
and know the temper of the world
enough to know they are waves breaking
more or less at the pace waves have
always broken. Provided you can still be in love
on a train with the woman whose hair
is dark and maned as the first night it tumbled
onto your skin. And sneak a little look
while she reads a book or dozes to the train's
rhythm. O, provided you can witness
for her sake the mile after mile of blossoming
whitethorns, the cattle grazing in one

direction, the slickly wet necks of horses
twisting a behemoth out of mist and imagination.
And suffer again your lifelong trick
of falling into the cloud-transforming heavens
while, away to the west, empress evening
trails dappled sleeves of sunshine and shadow
across the heather, and far and near
clumps of golden furze rich with the scent
of marzipan break your heart faithfully as ever.

Last Night a Starling

for Judy

You may imagine I'm off my head, unhinged by the days and nights
spent alone, but never was life so crowded or sociable
as here in the valley of clouds no sooner spilled than replenished.

The young oak forest starts everything off; assorted voices
of wind and rain, insect and bird, speak through its choppy verdure
which lengthens my gaze away towards Tullaroan's hills

before three goldfinches descend in full flight skimming sips
from a garden pool, and I am blinked back to lily-pads
with their 'linger on' sublime decay of turning ochre, fawn and lime.

A glut of frogspawn beginning to hatch into tadpoles
thickens among weeds, and the grey heron – known as an autumnal,
thieving visitor – is living meanwhile by the River Nore.

Tales from Norman Ireland, brought to book, summon me up
to a bed chamber where Petronella of Meath awakens
from her long-relinquished story. Petronella, servant girl six times

whipped senseless that she might confess to witchy practices,
burned at the stake, High Street 1363, no redress possible, and so many
wrongs down to our own time touted as virtuous or worthy

of emulation. But where, you might ask, is relief in this garden
made savage as it is beautiful – a blackbird playing
tug-o'-war with the earth before gobbling the extracted
    earthworm,

a cat plucking breast feathers from the robin he's caught
and coyly presenting it for my approval, or the fast-emerging
    tadpoles
permitted to fatten until the stand-offish heron comes

as if understanding when to take what is innocent and
    remorseless
as himself. No soft comforts underpin my green reverie,
the grass, the wildflower and the tree a twist away from
    something

terrible, still I send these words across the gap between us
to assert that we find beauty, even joy, opening afresh in the
    sudden,
fierce lives of nature blessed with its own argument and purpose.

I picture you mixing colours in your low attic studio
amid clutter of brushes, canvases, jars and rags, your daubed
    depictions
of old furniture falling down on its luck, drawing-rooms

full of faded grandeur and depth, or there's a heavy padlocked
    door,
sunshine through a casement blazoned on a landing floor.
Your brushstrokes take me back to the bockety armchair
    cushioned

with its accustomed crease, the tannin-stained teacup, the
    asparagus fern
seeming to levitate from its perch on top of the rusty cistern;
back to familiar haunts where we might linger behind the scenes

long after our lives have happened to us – subliminal, given to
    blending
with ornate wallpaper patterns or able to hide in hazes
of lamplight. I see your mouth sulk as you drowse beside the fire,

your hair unkempt, hand placed on hand – translucent gold. I
    stare
the bundled, baggy-trousered, smock-jumpered length
of you, all spattered and stained from your palette, and despite

the vicissitudes of our years together the only word that fits is
    'svelte'.
As for love or consummation of love, this becomes transmuted
to a soliloquy, a more vivid awareness of the daily mundane;
    alone,

I revert to the child of Callows solitude, who feels the wind
    freshening up,
who finds his every word flung back into his mouth,
stoppering his gullet until – somehow placated – he goes without,

as equally you must, shrinking these distances to an ache assuaged
by the thought that later we will more fiercely embrace, more
    fervently kiss.
And – a change of tenor or of tack – last night a starling
    fluttered

from behind a kitchen curtain, so scarifying me I threw my
   anorak
over the black flame of its flight and extinguished it sufficiently
   to feed out
to the bigger dark. The look of repose holding its countenance

as I loosed it haunted me through to light. But don't say an empty
mind's easily entertained, even if I tell you how ragwort
waves its yellow torches in my line of sight and that I never tire
   of this,

or if I admit to dwelling for hours on the crusty capsules of the
   cowslip,
or that I counter the quiet by talking to myself – the TV broken,
the radio whistling. All is a feasting, delicious, slow – on
   strawberries grown

sweeter for being wild and rare; on nights the black of your hair;
on dreams taking root under the wind and the palavering
raindrops in the poly-tunnel all afternoon; on 'damsel' and
   'dragonfly'

stop-overs gowned emerald or electric blue that happen by the
   water
composed, each towards her seeming standstill, her mid-air
faint; on cloud animals, bear becoming lion, lion turning
   crocodile;

on renaissance of light, God and bugling angel imaginable in
   sunburst soon,
or soon beyond an evening window the full moon. And do these
suffice, that salve my needful senses so? Do they replace you?
   Well, no.

NOTES

'Gallagh Man' is the name given to an Iron Age bog body, circa 470 – 200 BC, unearthed near Castleblakeney, Co Galway, in 1821. He was apparently kept 'under wraps' in the peat for some years, and uncovered on occasions for 'showing' to visitors.

What is generally regarded as the bloodiest battle in Irish history was fought on the 12th July 1691, between forces loyal to King James 1 and the armies of Prince William 111, in Aughrim, a village on the N6 between Ballinasloe and Loughrea.

A number of poems in the 'King of the Wood' section are versions of old Irish myths and legends associated with trees. Others were written following a reading of 'The Golden Bough' by James Frazier. Certain of the customs described by Frazier as having been practised during ancient times – for example the Maypole dance – still lingered during my childhood.

The Red Sash Brigade – lumberjack gangs working in America in the late 1800s – were notorious for their hard drinking and rowdy behaviour.

While I take liberty chronologically with it in the idea of its being worked by 'a great-great-grandfather's great-grandfather', the Addergoole Cot, found in Addergoole Bog, Lurgan, Co Galway, is the oldest intact Irish vessel, a huge log-boat hollowed out from the trunk of an oak tree, circa 2,500 B.C.

'The House of the Fire' is based on an account given by W.F. Wakeman, 19th Century antiquarian, of 'Leac na Tine', the Store of the Fire, on Inishmurray Island, off the coast of Co Sligo.

In 'Subterranean Song' the 'magnum opus' in question is Seumas O'Kelly's 'The Weaver's Grave'. The last vestiges of O'Kelly's maternal home could still be seen at my father's birthplace when I was a child.

'Golem' is a Hebrew word meaning 'rudiment', 'embryo', or simply 'raw material'. In Jewish folklore, the golem was said to be shaped from inanimate matter and given life that it might serve its creator.

'Drowning machine' is a term used to describe the whirlpool effect discernible at the base of a waterfall.

Tynagh Mine, Co Galway, was one of Europe's richest lead, silver and zinc mines. It commenced production in 1965 and closed down in 1981.

Gaelic words and phrases occur in a number of poems. In 'Emigrant', 'lán dóchais' meaning 'full of hope', and 'le ciúnas gan chrá' meaning 'quietly without torment', are taken from 'Mise Raifeirí an File' by Antoine Ó Raifteirí, the blind 18th century poet and fiddler born in Killeadan, Co Mayo, who spent most of his life in and around south Co Galway.

The word 'sleán', occurring in the poems 'Gallagh Man' and 'Panache', is a spade-like implement used for cutting turf.

'Sliotar' is a hurling ball, 'cuileog' a fly, 'tráithnín' a grass stalk, and 'gabháil' an armful (of hay, straw or turf).

'Cailleach', meaning 'hag' or 'crone', also has designations as 'wise woman', 'deity' and 'deified ancestor'. The poem here is based on a legend of how the outcrop of rock named for the Cailleach at Beara Peninsula, Co Cork, came to exist.

'Seanchaí', as in 'The Last Seanchaí', is a traditional storyteller, and the house where people visited to listen to his stories was called a 'rambling' house.

'Fear bréige' is a construct of timber and rags made to resemble a person and stood in a field in the perhaps vain hope that it might deter crows and other birds from eating the farmer's crops.

Milton Keynes UK
Ingram Content Group UK Ltd.
UKHW010727061223
433851UK00001B/46